SIMPLIFY YOUR HOME, SIMPLIFY YOUR LIFE

ZERO-CLUTTER HOME & UNSTUFF YOUR HOME
2 IN 1 MINIMALISM BUNDLE - HOW TO
DECLUTTER AND TIDY UP YOUR HOME, LIVE A
MEANINGFUL LIFE, AND FIND SIMPLICITY,
INNER JOY AND FREEDOM (A MINIMALIST
GUIDE FOR BEGINNER)

LILLY NOLAN

FREE GIFT!

Do you want a checklist that can help you tidy up your home in only one week?

In order to thank you for reading my book, I've included a 7-day declutter checklist for you. This printable cheat sheet will help you clean your home room-by-room easily!

Get yours now >> https://dl.bookfunnel.com/jbyr5w8qpf

CONTENTS

ZERO-CLUTTER HOME

UNSTUFF YOUR HOME

ZERO-CLUTTER HOME

MINIMALIST STRATEGIES TO SIMPLIFY
YOUR LIFE, ORGANIZE YOUR HOME ROOM
BY ROOM, DECLUTTER YOUR MIND, AND
CREATE A FOCUSED AND MEANINGFUL
LIFE

INTRODUCTION

When it comes to the interior of your home, it is only natural that you would want everything to be perfect. After all, it is your home! With that said, we occasionally find ourselves struggling and what we end up having is a house that is far too congested. Surely, it didn't seem that way when we started, did it?

I know, I've been there. Trying to achieve this so-called perfection led me to buy almost anything I wanted. It was only after it was too late that I realized I spent quite a lot of money on things that I may never even use. Not the kind of situation we would want to be in, I know I don't. However, learning from this experience of mine, I analyzed my mistakes, did a bit of research and came up with ideas that certainly impacted my way of living. If it helped me, why should I keep this information to myself?

For years, I have been providing tips and solutions to a lot of people I know personally. These methods and techniques have gone on to change their lifestyles completely.

Having a minimalist home carries quite a lot of perks. Not only are you saving yourself from excess clutter, you are promoting better living habits, improving your mental and physical state, and creating a place where everyone would feel inspired and welcomed.

If you have just bought yourself your very own house and are eager to start decorating the place, you are in luck! Let this book help you out in ensuring you do not end up in a cluttered atmosphere. Let this book be a guide to you and to anyone who may already have a house and wish to bring new life to the place, add character, charm, and personality to the house. Welcome to "Minimalist Home," where we learn how to convert any house into a living, breathing, and inviting home.

What you'll find in this book

This is perhaps the million-dollar question you had when you decided to have a look through this book. I have given this a fair thought and decided on a few things which would help develop an understanding while keeping things as easy and simple as possible.

To get the maximum benefits out of this book, you do not need any prior knowledge. I will try and ensure no jargon is used that may cause you to look it up as my goal is to share my experience with the masses, and offer an understanding of how they can switch from a crowded place to a minimalist setup that is both attractive and elegant in nature.

The book will walk you through various steps. We will

try to cover each section of the house one by one. I will guide you through what is needed and what isn't. Expect a few clarifications and questions which will help you realize the difference between 'want' and 'need' as these can get a little tricky.

The book is carefully structured to ensure you keep pace and know exactly where we are and where we will be going in the next chapter. Some of these changes might be quite challenging at first, especially if you let your sentiments get in the way. Don't worry though, I will guide you through on how to overcome such moments.

The first time I was asked to get rid of a few things I personally picked out for my desk, I was furious. It took a little time to do so but I am glad that I did it. Now, my desk is only a space for things which I truly use. It immediately started feeling more comfortable and 'roomy' because all that clutter on my desk made me feel like I was in a corporate office. I could never gain the peace of mind that I need in order to carry out my work.

The journey to a minimalist home begins with firstly understanding the core concept of minimalism and how it helps us lead a better, healthier and more peaceful life. The journey will put you to the test initially. What you need to remember is that you are not doing this to quit. I can rest you assure that by the time you are done reading this book, you will be eager to get started on working with ideas and feel the change in the air around you. You will have all the confidence in the world you need to do what you may have perceived as "too hard" or even downright impossible.

Things to Keep an Eye Out For

I truly and genuinely wish to engage with you to create a world where we can visualize what your perfect minimalist home would look like. Therefore, I will provide some mental exercises at points to keep you engaged. You will see the difference it makes when I ask you to change the position of a table, or tidy up smaller items which are just lying around in your house that serve no true purpose. The facts will eventually come to you and you will be surprised to find out just how much space these little things can consume for no reason at all.

The book will also provide you with scenarios where you can use the knowledge you gain from this book and apply it on your own. Undoubtedly, there is no such thing as a perfect strategy. Perfection might be a different concept for you, but the principle remains the same. Using these scenarios, you will eventually develop an understanding to start looking at things through the eye of a minimalist and see just how you can improve your own living space and make it feel alive and inviting instead of dreary and dark. With that said, let us dive straight into the book and embark on a journey to see what the fuss is all about.

1

JUST WHAT IS MINIMALISM ANYWAY?

"Simplicity is the ultimate sophistication."

LEONARDO DA VINCI

Before we can dive into the world of minimalist homes, there are a few things that are essential to understand and digest from here on out. Without these basic concepts, the entire book would feel hollow and meaningless.

I will give you a few minutes to ponder and come up with an explanation of what you think minimalism is. You can use a pen and paper to jot down whatever you think is the true definition. Once you are done, let's move on to contemplate minimalism in greater detail.

Minimalism is the art of understanding and identifying the essentials and discarding the rest. There is always a point where we feel the need to have more, but often, for whatever reason, the urge can be to gather more of things that we do not actually need. In subscribing to a minimalist attitude, a minimalist way of life, you will be attempting to live more simply. Go minimalist and you will find yourself embracing a less cluttered way of life that often brings a greater sense of freedom, calm and satisfaction.

Does that all sound a little vague? Let me tell you a little more of my story. I am a minimalist, a person who lives a simple, healthy, and fun lifestyle by detaching myself from all that is unnecessary and sticking to the essentials. I have, over the years, learned how to easily master the art of minimalism and differentiate between what I 'want' and what I 'need,' and that is something which a lot of people end up getting wrong. Do not confuse minimalism with being miserable, or being frugal and not willing to spend a dime on luxuries. It is not that! If anything, **I am living with less to create room for more.**

There are quite a few examples that I can quote, and almost immediately you will be able to relate to them. The reason for this is that smaller things are easy to ignore, but they can eventually pile up into a clutter-zone that will get in the way of us working or even moving about. Things such as newspapers, disposable cans and cups, and pretty much anything that is not meant to be there will only add to the misery and the clutter.

The problem most people face is that they are not able to identify what exactly they should get rid of and what they should continue to keep. There is no clear line that we draw for ourselves to help us make that decision. The inability to make such a decision then creates room for physical clutter. We keep on purchasing everything that we may think we need and start piling them up with the rest. Before you know it, you will have a pile of things that are gathering dust instead of attention. If you know you do not need something, don't invest in it. If you are reading this book then the chances are good that you are already surrounded by unnecessary things. Minimalism gives us the confidence to let these things go.

My Take On a "Minimalist Home"

Hopefully, by now, the concept of minimalism is somewhat clear. Now, apply the same to a complete house, and you have a minimalist home. A structure that only houses the essentials is what you end up with. Of course, everyone has a different perspective. Strikes one person as minimalist may strike another as cluttered. I found that my perspective shifted with each stage of my journey into minimalism. My take on a minimalist home is based on years of research, and my understanding and application of the concept itself, and would include the following:

- Lots of comfortable space
- Bright lights (natural or otherwise)
- A simple layout
- Ease of movement
- Good storage
- Essential items
- Plants (trust me on this one)

In my world, these seemingly little things matter a lot as they have this great ability to amplify the available space and make everything look much more pleasing and appealing. With these minimalist essentials, every time I walk through the front door I know I will encounter a simple and welcoming atmosphere. My minimalist home instantly re-energizes me so I am ready to enjoy the evening after a long day at work.

If this is what you are looking for, but find it difficult to remove items from your life, the first step is to systematically go through each room in your house or apartment. Make a note of each item that either no longer has a purpose in your home, or perhaps never did. These are items that you may want to get rid of when the time comes. We all have different relationships with our things and the process of getting rid of things is not always an easy one. There will no doubt be things that you will immediately be able to stuff into a bag for the trash, or eBay, but for other things, you may need to get used to the idea of not seeing it anymore. Making that list is a good way of getting yourself used to no longer having that item of sentimental value in your life. It's important to understand that minimalism is a process and preparing yourself psychologically is the first step.

In the next chapter, I will provide you with a little exercise to fully enable you to learn what you need to get rid of and what you need to keep. We will also come across a fact that might surprise you. Keep those ideas flowing for now, write and come back when you are ready to move ahead!

The Takeaway

- Minimalism is the process by which we identify what we need as opposed to what we want. The two are not always the same, often we keep things that no longer serve a real purpose.
- Everyone has their own unique view of what a minimalist home is. Your home doesn't need to look like mine. The principle of minimalism remains the same.
- Physical clutter can consume a lot of space and impact your quality of life. Having more space should make way for more of what makes you happy, not clutter.
- For items that are difficult to imagine getting rid of, make a list as the first step towards being comfortable with the idea.

2

HOARDER - ARE YOU ONE?

"It is preoccupation with possession, more than anything else, that prevents men from living freely and nobly."

BERTRAND RUSSELL

Most of you may have read the title of this chapter and may have already come to a conclusion, thinking: "Surely, I can't be a hoarder, can I?" There is definitely no rule that states that you need to be a hoarder in order to reap the benefits of minimalism, and I am not saying that you are definitely a hoarder, but it is a habit that one can easily pick up without even realizing.

Firstly, what exactly is a hoarder? Sure, we have all heard the term and maybe come across a TV show about zany characters who have packed their homes full of seem-

ingly useless junk. Now you're thinking back to those TV
shows and thinking: "Well, that's definitely not me." Well,
you don't need to be an extreme hoarder like that in order
to be considered a hoarder. Let's take a few moments to go
through some of the key tell-tale signs that could identify
one as a hoarder.

Do you:

- find it impossible to throw away belongings?
- become anxious when trying to dispose of
  items?
- have difficulty in organizing your belongings?
- feel overwhelmed by your belongings?
- become concerned about others touching your
  possessions?
- worry obsessively about running out of an item,
  or needing it in the future?
- find it difficult to move around your home?
- experience relationship difficulties with those
  close loved ones?

If you have felt a connection with any of these, it is
possible that you are a hoarder, but are reluctant to admit it.
This is only natural as most people are not keen on radical
changes to behavior and habits. It is only when the transition is made that we realize how much we were holding
back. Time for a quick breather. Let this newly found information sink in. It is quite a discovery, isn't it?

Why do you think I am constantly focusing on space
and clutter? It has everything to do with my own experi-

ences. I used to procrastinate a lot. There came a time where it started having an effect on my mental and physical state. It affected the way I worked, the way I felt, and worse, it affected my relationships. Believe it or not, being surrounded by clutter does have drastic effects. This is one reason why one often feels comfort and a sense of tranquility when entering a hotel room.

A lot of people consider themselves the opposite of being a hoarder; only a select few may have stopped to reconsider, but this is a process that we all have to go through.No one said that the path to minimalism is an easy one, but we are trying to look at the bigger picture here, aiming to create a home and a life that has everything we need, instead of things that we merely desire. The shift in mindset can be quite difficult, but one that will surely have a positive impact on your life.

The 90/90 Rule

Do you still have that pen and paper with you? Good, because you'll need it.

Let us revisit your list and see how many of the things you decided to jot down you think are consuming space. It could be that big armchair you never use, the rather massive lamps occupying more space than they need; it could be anything that doesn't actually serve a productive purpose. If your list is already crowded, good job! On the other hand, if you have only written a thing or two, you might be having a hard time deciding what to let go of due to the sentiments attached to those items. Don't worry, I have just the exercise for that.

This exercise is one that I personally found really helpful. It is based on a 90/90 rule. The objective is simple; for every object that you own, ask yourself two questions:

- Have I used this in the last 90 days?
- Will I use it in the next 90 days?

If your answer is "no", that object should be going in a box to depart your home for good. This exercise may take a little while, but rest assured, you will be staggered to discover how many things around your home fall into neither of the two above categories. Don't cop out and get bogged down by the 'probablys' or 'maybes'. If you haven't used something, the chances are very good that you won't use that item at all. It is best to get rid of it and create some space.

Going from room to room, this exercise may take some time, but it is definitely time well spent as it puts you in a great position to your minimalism journey a successful one. Be strict with yourself and keep in mind the question: "Am I a hoarder?" You might find your answer changes.

Once again, grab your pen and paper, and now with this added knowledge, start jotting down things you think are worthy to be removed but you feel as though you can't as you may have sentimental value attached to them. If you haven't already realized, you are creating this list to ease your decision making once the time comes.

Sure, the exercise above is a great way to discover just how many items are contributing to the clutter in your home, but in the next chapter we will look a little deeper into the benefits that decluttering can bring you. These are benefits which can change quite a lot, more than just the way your house looks. If you are going to make a success of your minimalism journey, it is essential that you understand the benefits that you stand to gain. This will keep you motivated through the difficult parts that can be emotional for those who have real sentimental feelings for their possessions.

The Takeaway

So, to recap, here's what we have learned in this chapter:

- There are many signs that you may be a hoarder. Worrying about running out of things, relationship difficulties due to your possessions, anxiety about throwing things out... these are all signs.
- Being a hoarder can have a huge impact upon your life, but you do not need to be a hoarder to adopt a minimalist lifestyle and reap the benefits.
- The negativity around hoarding is about more than just the physical space it takes up in your home. Hoarding can seriously affect your state of mind and your outlook on life.
- Adopt the 90/90 rule to determine whether an item should go to a better home, or stay put.

Have you used an item in the last 90 days? If not, do you anticipate using it in the next 90 days? If the answer to both these questions is "no", the item should go.

- Preparation is key to support you through the difficult periods on your minimalism journey. That's why it is a good idea to go from room to room and prepare the path for the journey ahead.

3

BENEFITS OF DECLUTTERING YOUR HOME - PSYCHOLOGICAL AND BEYOND!

"Smile, breathe and go slowly."

THICH NHAT HANH

Well, there is no denying the fact that there is a fine line between 'collecting' and cluttering. However, people still get confused between the two, and it is easy to see why.

An item that you 'collect' holds a monetary or sentimental value and is ideally kept in pristine condition. It is stored in an organized fashion. Clutter is just about everything else that has no order, no organized thought behind it. The items may have a monetary value but if it is not serving any purpose as such and is just lying around, it is considered part of clutter.

The reason I made this point here is because I have

noticed quite a lot of people who, when told to clear up clutter, immediately come up with an excuse. Again, it is natural, I do not blame you at all if you end up using "I'm collecting these" as an excuse. Things that have to go cannot remain. Remember the 90/90 rule we discussed earlier? If the item you are 'collecting' has served no purpose or has not been used in the last 90 days, it's time to say goodbye, unless they are gaining monetary value and providing genuine value.

Why you should declutter

Let's quickly go through the reasons why decluttering not only makes sense, but will also make you feel good about yourself, impacting areas of your life that you hadn't even considered. Decluttering:

1. improves your confidence
2. makes you feel re-energized
3. can help to reduce anxiety
4. encourages physical activity
5. reduces tension around relationships
6. helps you to rediscover lost items

Decluttering takes a bit of time and some genuine will. You cannot expect to get up today and rid your house of all the things which consume both space and room. It is a process, which is a good thing since we can use that time to recollect our thoughts and refocus our priorities. You may have already compiled a list of items to get rid of, but you should expect additional entries once you start decluttering.

There is no such thing as a "good time" to start. You can begin right now if you prefer. Your first step, small or big, inaugurates your will to begin decluttering and reaping the benefits. Let's take a closer look at those benefits I mentioned earlier.

Decluttering improves your confidence

In taking the decision to declutter your home you have already made a major life decision. This alone is hugely empowering, but it only counts if you follow through with your mission. To do this you will need to make a raft of other decisions along the way. Not only will you be deciding what to remove from your home, but you will also need to decide how to remove those items. Which pile of items will go to goodwill, which will go to be sold at a yard sale, which will end up on eBay. Aside from that, you will also need to decide where the remaining items will go in your home and how they will fit into your existing storage space.

It may sound overwhelming to read about all these decisions that you need to make. Perhaps part of the issue that led to accumulating so much clutter was that you have trouble making decisions, so reading about how you will need to make decisions may not sound like good news. But it is! Making decisions, and sticking to them, will help you to feel confident and empowered. Making decisions makes you feel like you are in charge of your own life, and perhaps for the first time in a long time you will feel like you own the items you are getting rid of, they no longer own you.

Decluttering makes you feel re-energized

Once you begin to make decisions, you will soon find that you are ready to make all sorts of other decisions. Humans are natural problem-solvers and we do find ourselves stimulated by the process of thinking things through and coming up with solutions that will make our lives better. The fact that you are reading this book means that you have already identified a need to streamline your life and get a grip on your environment. In picking up this book you have already made a decision, and as you take onboard the advice and suggestions here you are unconsciously getting yourself prepared to take further action. The next steps you take will leave you feeling re-energized and ready to take on bigger challenges in your life.

Decluttering can help to reduce anxiety

Humans have a natural inclination towards creating and maintaining order. When things feel disordered it can leave us feeling lost in our own homes, creating anxiety that reduces our happiness. Begin the process of decluttering and you will soon find your anxiety and stress levels lowering as your place of rest and relaxation becomes less cluttered and less "busy" with items.

There was a time when I used to loathe the idea of coming back home. It always seemed to be stuffed and had these negative vibes and a dull interior, despite the fact that I spent quite a while picking out the best furniture. Now, after having my new-found love-affair with minimalism, I cannot find a better place anywhere else.

Decluttering encourages physical activity

I'm not saying that you need to hit the gym more often, or need to get more physical exercise, but most of us could do with getting more active. Decluttering your home is a great way to get some more exercise as you move around a lot more, going from room to room, organizing items into piles, lifting from one place to another, taking boxes and bags out to the car to take to goodwill, etc.

The act of physical activity means that you also have time to think about other things. Our typical days commandeer so much of our thoughts for work-related topics and issues that we do not often have the opportunity to really consider our lives and relationships. It is important that we do not take these things for granted and decluttering is an activity that requires thought and decision-making, but also leaves room for other thoughts to percolate.

Decluttering reduces tension around relationships

If your relationships with those who live with you have been under strain because of the clutter in your life, decluttering is a great way to let them know that you do listen to them and that you are taking onboard their views. Even if you are not arguing about the mess, the stress in your relationship could be manifesting itself in different ways, with arguments about other things. Decluttering may not eliminate those arguments altogether, but it will help to reduce the stress in the household and make for a more pleasant atmosphere. Have you ever found yourself annoyed that you cannot find your car keys because of the clutter? Imagine being able to find everything when you need it, no need to hunt around. It would leave you in a better frame of mind and less inclined to snap at others.

My relationships have also improved dramatically. No longer do I engage in quarrels over petty things with my partner at home. The lights we have used have greatly boosted our mood and always provide us with comfort. My work habits have greatly increased as well. I can now focus on what I need to do without being distracted by piles of papers, books, and empty plates on the workstation.

Decluttering helps you to rediscover lost items

Sort through the clutter and you may find yourself digging out items that you had previously thought lost for all time. I know, the idea is to get rid of things, not to find additional things that you want to keep. However, I am talking about useful things that you won't need to buy because you already have them. It is not uncommon to discover unexpired medication or other useful items that you had thought were lost or had clean forgotten about. Finding items in this way gives you a good feeling like you have gotten lucky and won a tiny lottery. This can put you in a good mood and leave you eager to tackle bigger piles of clutter.

Reflecting back, the first thing I removed from my premises were my old clothes. I had tons of clothes and frankly, there came a point where I realized I had no room left for new ones. I knew I had to take some steps to address the situation. To everyone's surprise, I had gotten to the point where I had to use a few chests of drawers to store my old clothes. It only took a second for me to realize I was being a pack rat here.

With a heavy heart, I decided to donate more than half of my old clothes. Surely, someone else would need them more than I needed them. Now, I had more room and my wardrobe didn't feel like all the clothes would burst out the minute I opened it. It felt nice.

This initial feeling is what drove me to rethink everything. I started getting rid of old furniture which was nothing more than a waste of space. I then moved towards other smaller things and before I realized it, I had a home that felt spacious and bright; I couldn't believe it.

This newly found hobby of mine turned into a passion. I knew this started affecting my lifestyle. Apparently, the impact was profound and prominent which is what led a friend of mine from the neighborhood to ask me to have a look around his house and provide him with some suggestions. Now, his house is a beautiful place, full of energy, great vibes, and light.

The Takeaway

A quick recap of things on what we learned in this chapter:

- There is a difference between collecting and cluttering. collecting can be about holding on to things that may have already have value, or have value in the future. Clutter is all the stuff that has no real value and will not appreciate in value with time.

- There is no such thing as an 'ideal' time to start decluttering your home It may always feel like an arduous task to begin. The only way to start is to actually start. Don't make excuses, just get on with it.

- Once you begin decluttering you will begin to feel a new sense of confidence as you begin making decisions and taking control.

- Humans love to solve problems, we find it stimulating, so do not be surprised to find yourself feeling re-energized by the process of decluttering.

- The more you declutter the greater the feeling of general wellness. You will find your levels of anxiety dropping as you take charge, make decisions and begin seeing the space in your life again.

- Not only does the activity of decluttering mean that you will be getting more physical exercise, but your mind will have the freedom to wander, giving you more time for your thoughts.

- Decluttering will not only help you to reduce your levels of anxiety, but also those of others around you. You will find yourselves snapping less and being more relaxed around one another. Not only that but through the process of decluttering you may also discover items that you had previously thought lost.

And that's a wrap for this chapter. As promised, we will now be moving towards more practical parts of the book, starting with the kind of mindset a minimalist should have.

4

THE MINIMALIST MINDSET

"Reduce the complexity of life by eliminating the needless wants of life, and the labors of life reduce themselves."

EDWIN WAY TEALE

With all the talk about decluttering and getting rid of stuff that we don't need; it does sound like minimalism is all about throwing everything away while surviving on the bare minimum. That is not the case. Instead, minimalism is adapting to a change in lifestyle and living with things which are necessary, giving away those that are not, and hence creating room for other things to come. It is to get rid of excess and favor the important stuff. That, as a result, allows you to find fulfillment, happiness, and a lot of freedom.

Minimalism is not just limited to redoing your house and decluttering things, there is a lot more to it than this. Minimalism is a mindset, a genuinely intriguing way of thinking which brings life-altering results.

You can have quite a lot of money, a massive house, a bit of fame, and almost every desirable item, but even after that, you may never feel fulfilled. If the answer to life was this simple, every one of us would function in a completely different way.

A minimalistic mindset allows you to seek out only the important aspects in life and let go of those which hold no value or are just temporarily serving a purpose. By holding something important close to you, you are giving the appropriate attention without being divided or distracted by other things. Your family, your friends, your social life - everything improves for the better.

The best bit about this is that once you adopt this mindset and start analyzing things for what they are, you will find your savings increasing twice as fast as they did before. Now, you will no longer be spending money on unnecessary items and will learn to make do with what you need and what you already have.

As a minimalist, ask yourself questions constantly. Are you buying this because you 'may' one day need it or are you buying this because you will definitely need it? A minimalist never invests in anything he/she isn't sure about. This allows them to maintain focus on what is essential and important while overlooking all which aren't. It is hard, I won't lie. The temptation to buy things often gets the best of us but once you train your mind not to give in to temptations, you will be relieved by the results.

Surely, there are things in life that you can still continue to buy such as clothes, however, your new mindset would allow you to easily decide what clothes you wish to give away that you already have to create room for the ones that are to come.

As long as you have a will to change your old habits, you have nothing to fear. It does take a little time for you to develop this new lifestyle, so don't rush into making these decisions and expect everything to change overnight. Allow it to settle in your mind and allow the change to flow through your body as well. Decluttering is just the first step towards minimalism. One of the biggest, but also the easiest areas to begin is with your clothes. We all cling on to items of clothing that no longer fit us. Sure, there are items that may fit us once more, but the chances are high that in the back of your closet there are things that can be used by someone else. Clothes take up a huge amount of space, but because we can make easy decisions about their fates based on how they fit us and whether they are still in style. You don't have to begin with your clothes, but it is a great way to feel like you have easily made a big impact.

The hallmark of a true minimalist is that they always enjoy whatever they own, fancy or otherwise. There is absolutely nothing that will make them feel left out if there is something out in the market, or in fashion, that they don't have. If we start letting things and trends control us, we aren't exactly living a free life then, are we?

Minimalism allows you to take your life back by the

reigns and drive it towards the direction you wish to pursue. Once you have control, you can now decide what comes into your home and what stays out of it. Of course, that sofa set you looked at seems like a fashionable addition, but if the one you already have is serving its purpose nicely, why change it? Learn how to be strict about allowing certain items within your home and standing up against those which are absolutely unnecessary. Not only would they cost you money, they would once again start cluttering your space.

What about storage?

Like I said, minimalism isn't about throwing stuff away or donating almost everything to other people. Needless to say, there are things you still need and would like to latch on to. Minimalism is incomplete without storage. In fact, through minimalism, you also learn how to effectively store your material items safely and in ways that they do not require more space than they need.

I have seen people using large boxes just to occupy a quarter of its capacity with clothes or children's toys. Again, why? Why use a box that is far too big for something that only requires a quarter of the space? It makes no sense. What does make sense then is to go for a smaller, stylish storage unit.

For clothes you can use a vacuum bag. Using these you can either press the air right out of the clothes and bag, or you can use a vacuum cleaner to suck the air right out of them. This is ideal if you have lots of thick winter clothes that you want to pack away for nine months out of the year. If you are looking for a storage solution that will be in plain sight, then find something that feels right and that would compliment the minimalist theme we are seeking out for your house. Don't use a large box for a few small items. Use a small box, or reevaluate whether you need those few small items. If not, remove them from your life. Remember that in purchasing a large storage solution you are preparing for future clutter, so don't do it! Only take on the storage that you really need. Once done, stick to it and use it well.

Always keep in mind that you are trying to declutter, not find storage solutions for the clutter you have. That is the opposite of decluttering.

Minimalism works differently for each and every one of us. There is no "one size fits all" method which we often try and seek out. Everyone has a different starting point and ending point. We all have things we find essential and we all have our personal preferences to consider. Depending on what your definition of minimalism is, stick to it and stop comparing yourself to others.

The best thing to do is to find a minimalism solution that works best for you. There is no one particular way to be a minimalist. The main thing is that you are streamlining your life and ditching all the things that you don't really need, improving your life and letting more space into it.

The Takeaway

Let us look back at some important things we learned and discussed in this chapter:

- Minimalism is a journey that you have to undertake, but it will only be a success if you adopt the minimalist mindset.
- The minimalist mindset is all about discarding the unnecessary and keeping old of only what is essential. This is true of all things, not just physical items around your home.
- Minimalism is not about getting rid of everything, be sensible, remove from your life only the things that are no longer needed. Buy and keep only what will bring you happiness and you will find that minimalism will save you money and time
- Minimalism allows us to regain control over our life, helps us develop better relationships.
- Make sure that your storage solutions work well with your minimalist aesthetic. Don't get rid of lots of stuff only to replace it with a bulky box that takes up as much space.

I will be seeing you back in the next chapter where we try and answer a common question I get asked every now and then. Why is it hard to declutter?

5

WHY IS IT DIFFICULT TO DECLUTTER?

"The ability to simplify means to eliminate the unnecessary so that the necessary may speak."

HANS HOFMANN

"I really don't know!" Believe me, this was my answer when I asked myself this very question. I read everything I needed, I had all the motivation in the world, but I just couldn't bring myself to carry out the decluttering process.

Most of you, the readers, will be facing the same thing right about now. Some of you might even be thinking that you will hopefully not face any problems when you start decluttering. The problem is, if you haven't already begun, you will only find it harder to do so later on.

Decluttering is an exercise in itself. It can be a challenge as there is quite a lot of decision-making required. However, I have already provided you with a solid starting point. That should provide you with some direction and give you a great idea of how simple things can be if you begin in the right way, with the right minimalist mindset.

Over the years, I have encountered various people and situations where they promise to start decluttering, only to end up procrastinating. When asked why, they provide various justifications and answers which always sound convincing. If we start to do that, we are lying to ourselves and barring ourselves from a life that is potentially healthy, stress-free, and enjoyable.

Common Excuses and Solutions to Them

Excuses are everywhere. We tend to come up with these in our daily lives. This leads us to ask how can we move past the excuses we always seem to come up with and truly begin decluttering?

Let us look at some of these excuses and try to find solutions to these statements that are barring us from moving forward.

I JUST DON'T HAVE the time to do it right now – Sure, we are all busy with our work duties for most of the day. Then, we try and strike a balance by spending some time with the family after work. It all sounds good, but if you are trying to bring about change, you have to stop and create the time you need to start decluttering. I can't urge you enough to do this. It is only the first time that you may find it difficult. The more you declutter, the easier it gets.

IT JUST FEELS LIKE A LOT – If you are overwhelmed by the idea of taking everything out to identify what goes back in and what goes out the door, it is only natural. However, do not let that get to you. There is nothing to be afraid of or intimidated about. Approach the process by breaking it down into chunks. There is no rush to get it all done in one day. Break each room down into separate tasks. Not only will it feel more manageable, but you will feel as though you are making swifter progress.

I MIGHT NEED this in the future – Let us be honest here for a while and think this through. How many times have we relied on projections about "the future" that just never seem to come true? If that day has yet to come, it is probably never coming your way. Let it go and stop delaying things. You are only piling things up as you wait for that 'maybe' to become a reality. If you aren't happy about donating it, see if you can sell it. Get some cash value back. It's a lot better than keeping something you will never use.

THIS WAS A GIFT – Gifts do have a sentimental value, I fully admit. However, in order to become a true minimalist, you need to analyze your gifts as well. Is this gift relevant to your situation right now? Is it serving any purpose? If your answer is no, it is okay to let this go as well. If you have quite a lot of shoes that you wear, and you have a pair that you haven't worn in over a year, say goodbye and let someone else who may need a pair wear these. Trust me, if you donate things that are useful, the sheer joy and peace you get for helping someone out is far greater than hoarding stuff.

THIS REMINDS me of (insert memory or person here) – Having to move on is sad, but it is life. I have seen people store furniture, clothes and even larger objects because they remind them of someone they may have lost. Keeping these will not bring them back and thus they are not serving you any purpose. If you truly love this person, you don't need items and garments to remember them by. Find another way to preserve your memories and clear these out. Let them become a source of happiness for someone else.

THERE ARE TOO many sentiments involved – This is broadly similar to the point above. I am sure you already get the point here as well. Sentiments can and do cloud our judgment. It is best to let such items go which have a tendency of making you cry, feel anxious, or even go silent. Your home should be a tower of positivity. Let all the negativity, sadness, and worries stay out of it.

. . .

WHY WASTE ANYTHING? – I am never going to suggest you waste anything. However, there is a fine line between wasting something and having stuff move on for a good cause. For example, the armchair that sits in the corner of your living room that no one seems to use, is giving that away considered wasting? If anything, that would be a favor you are doing to yourself and to your house. It was wasting the space that could have been taken up by something else. Start rethinking items you consider potentially wasted against those which are wastage themselves.

IT'S NOT ME, it's my partner – I don't really hear this often but I would be lying if I said I hadn't heard this before. People either blame each other or they may be truly trying to get rid of something while their partner seems to disagree. Approach your partner and discuss what you are trying to do and how it would greatly impact your lives and the environment of the house itself. Talking always helps and there is a good chance you two might agree upon letting such things go.

WITH ALL OF THESE EXCUSES, the common enemy was to delay matters. Excuses are made to create this false world to avoid responsibility and delay the matter for a later stage. There is no later stage; if you need to get something done, get it done today! Regardless of the excuse, take action. The first step is always the hardest, what follows is half as hard, and then the chain continues to get easier and easier.

The time has come for you to decide if you wish to stick to excuses or take action for a change. Remember the list we worked on in the first few chapters where you noted down all the most obvious things that you wanted to get rid of? Here's a bit of an exercise for you. Start decluttering at least a quarter of your items and just let them go. Take all the time you need because by the time you are done, you would be reading the next chapter with a new-found energy and positivity which would only push you to go forward.

In the next chapter, we will be looking at how we can deal with sentiments and ensure they don't get in the way of us making life-changing decisions. We will look at some examples and hopefully arrive at a conclusion on how to deal with this effectively.

The Takeaway

In this chapter, we learned the following things:

- We often have a habit of coming up with excuses. Excuses and minimalism cannot co-exist. Excuses are just another way to shift blame and delay matters
- Overcome excuses by taking the plunge and making a start. The first step is the most important, letting go of certain items is okay and there's nothing to be ashamed about.

- There is no ideal time to start, there will always be something else that you need to do before the time is "perfect". It can feel overwhelming at first, but take it one little step at a time.

- If it is your partner who is holding you back, sit down with them and have a frank conversation about how your quality of life is being affected. Explain to them how your lives would benefit from decluttering.

- No one is suggesting that you waste things, but there is a difference between wasting useful items and filling your home with useless waste.

- Certain items stir emotions within us and it can be difficult to remove those items from the home. Try to only keep items that stir up positive memories and feelings. My advice is to try to remove from your home items that only conjure up negativity.

- Be critical about gifts. Yes, they can hold sentimental value, but if they do not serve a purpose then they are just holding you back on your minimalism journey. The same goes for items you think might be useful at some point in the future. Stop holding on to things that might be useful one day.

6

DON'T LET SENTIMENTALITY GET IN THE WAY

"As you simplify your life, the laws of the universe will be simpler; solitude will not be solitude, poverty will not be poverty, nor weakness weakness."

HENRY DAVID THOREAU

When we talk about objects having sentimental value, we don't necessarily limit these sentiments to items that were gifted or left by someone we loved who may have moved on or passed away. There are items that we have special attachments to, things that we collect, and things that we have worked far too hard to give away. These can be as big as vehicles and houses to as small as stamps, stickers, model cars, and so on. If you were immediately asked to get rid of these, you might lose your temper right away. However, breathe easy; I am not asking you to do that.

I have met people throughout my life who have decluttered quite a lot of things and have made room within their house and apartments. With that said, there are always some items such as a guitar, a picture frame of a beloved person, or a collection of model cars which they will never get rid of. It is perfectly understandable. While that may seem okay, it is still necessary for you to see things from a neutral perspective.

If the collection of items are neatly organized and not consuming space, and or they have a monetary value, it is probably a good idea to keep them. Anything that falls out of this category, regardless of how much sentimental value it holds, is best to let go. If life teaches us anything, it is that everything, good or bad, must come to an end. Keeping something to remember someone by will not exactly serve a purpose. I shed a little light in the previous chapter about this - if you truly love someone, you don't need material items to remind you of them.

Yes, we do love those fond memories spent at the beach on a warm Sunday afternoon. Yes, we love to remind ourselves how great that trip across Europe was with our loved ones. But really, have we limited our memories and thoughts to material items alone?

Sentiments are a major hurdle to overcome. I have advised quite a few people to seek help from their partners or family members or even friends to make the transition easier. Letting go of things of sentimental value can be tough, but it doesn't stay that way forever. By letting such things go, it does not and should not imply that you have lost the love or don't love the said person as much as you did before. That is just our mind playing tricks on us. Deep down, our love never fades. It is always there with you.

I, too, had quite a lot of things that I collected out of passion or because I wanted them to remember someone by. It took me some time to realize this wasn't the best way to preserve happy memories and that these things were just not making me feel any happier. They weren't protecting me nor were providing me with anything useful in return. I was just piling things up and creating clutter. Eventually, with a heavy heart, I let these items go, and immediately things changed. I felt happy that I did. I felt free as I was no longer reliant upon material items to remind me of others or to feel safe.

This is quite a common situation for those who have numerous fashionable clothing. Fashion is something quite a lot of us wish to keep up with, and that is a passion, a sentiment that we just don't seem to understand properly. Sure, it is nice to look and feel great, but that does not give us a license to buy expensive clothes just so we can wear them once or twice and then let them sit in our wardrobe for years. I asked someone to give away such articles and was immediately met with a frown. Holding on to such clothes which you 'may' wear again is just delaying the inevitable. You will either forget about these articles completely or outgrow them. If that doesn't apply, rest assured the fashion trends will change and render them outdated. Slice it any way you like; it is just clutter that is waiting to be cleared out.

Digitization is a minimalist's best friend

As harsh as this may sound, it can be true. When we attach sentiments to objects, this makes us do things we may normally never do. Objects are just objects; they will come and go. The minute we attach sentimental value to them, our mind immediately thinks that these items are important. Frankly, that does not change the state of the object at all. They will continue to take up space, sit around in some part of the house, and be forgotten about completely. It is only when someone asks you to get rid of these items that you look back and remember they were there.

You only live once. If you put a hold on life, by clinging on to items that hold sentimental value for you, you may be missing out on a lot of things that might make you feel more positive. Keep only what is essential. Everything else is easily classified as clutter. Again, this may sound harsh, but I am only suggesting you free yourself of the objects, not the happy memories.

The actual problem lies in how to hold onto the memories while getting rid of the physical objects. Let us not forget the fact that we live in the era of the internet, smartphones, and computers. Now, we have brilliant cameras and applications which can store perfect pictures of 3D objects and scan any essential documents that you may find useful. All of this can be done at a push of a button and stored in a space that would only take up a small portion of your pocket. Digitizing these makes far more sense than ever. It is understandable that letting things go is a little hard, but now you have the pictures and scans to help you relive the memories easily.

Digitizing objects, cards, pictures, toys, dresses, or even post-it notes can help you organize things a lot easier. Just imagine the sheer space you will now be able to clear up, without worrying if you would ever see these things again or not. You do not even need any specialized equipment in order to do this. Most of the smartphones in existence today will easily be able to capture high-resolution pictures. For documents, either use a scanner or hold it underneath a light source and take a picture from the top to store the content as a picture, without compromising readability.

Of course, there are some documents which cannot be discarded, but I would still advise you to keep scans for those, just for backup purposes. The entire exercise is relatively quick and easy. You would actually have fun doing this. The result would be a space that was waiting to come out.

Try to keep sentimental thoughts out of your mind when you start to declutter your house. It will genuinely help you overcome quite a lot of hurdles, and by the time you are done, you will see that you have much more out there to experience beyond the memories held by the objects in your home.

The Takeaway

This was probably a tricky one to digest. However, in the spirit of learning, let us look back at what this chapter was all about.

- Sentimental thoughts can stop us from freeing ourselves from our clutter.
- You do not need objects to remember people or special moments.
- Collecting things can be good if it is for a special interest, or a hobby, but too much of it and it can get out of hand.
- Digitizing objects and documents can greatly assist us by allowing us to hold onto the memory while allowing us to discard the object associated with it.
- Putting your sentimental thoughts aside will help if you wish to succeed as a minimalist

Coming up next is our first look into your minimalist home. We will look through some ideas to get that creativity flowing and get that curiosity going. We will look at what elements you can use to further enhance your experience as a minimalist.

7

THE KEY TO YOUR MINIMALIST HOME

"The secret of happiness, you see, is not found in seeking more, but in developing the capacity to enjoy less."

SOCRATES

It hasn't been long since you started reading this book, and already there must be ideas going through your head about how you would start decluttering, what kind of a house you envision as a perfect minimalist house, and so on. This is a good start. If you have already carried out your first duty of sorting of items and actually carried out some of the things which I mentioned in earlier chapters, well done!

Remember, minimalism is not just about getting rid of stuff. There are things we will continue to retain. The problem is that we may not know the correct way of storing them. Just piling them up in the corner of a room, hanging clothes on a railing inside the wardrobe, this is just another way of burdening your storage unit. There are things you should start doing to further improve the way you store your stuff, stuff like clothes, food items, wallets and bags, keys, etc.

There will surely come a time where you might start feeling like you are about to run out of space. If that happens, declutter a little more and get rid of things that have otherwise gathered dust instead of attention. What you lose today might be someone else's gain tomorrow. You can always donate these things to people who may need them a lot more than you do. The state of knowing that you did good for someone else without asking for anything in return is one that cannot be defined in words. Try it out yourself and see how wonderful it feels to know you were able to make a difference in someone's life.

Let us now proceed and take our first practical look into your house. Let us try and figure out what is wrong and what we can further take away to brighten up the place.

Let's Make Some Changes!

Let us start by observing a few things about how you live and then change a few habits. Remember, to change something, it can be done instantly, but to make it a habit, it does take time. Do not rush into it.

Are you someone who has quite a lot of stuff? Do you deem yourself a person who stores things in boxes thinking you might need them someday? Is your kitchen a mess despite all your finest efforts? You can fix all of that by thinking outside of the box and coming up with a nifty storage solution.

Storage plays a vital part in being a minimalist. The trick lies in identifying the right kind of storage that suits you and your needs. The only thing that remains constant is the principle of retaining things that are in use and that are important while removing the remainder as a part of decluttering.

I generally observe myself as a person who follows a one in, one out rule. For every single item that I bring to the home, I will make room by removing one item that is no longer in use or has served its complete purpose. Why should I or you or anyone else for the matter invest a fortune into increasing storage space every time you purchase things?

Our house is for us to live in while it also allows us to store our important things. If we were to use the entire house and stuff it with unnecessary items, it would defeat the purpose and push us out instead.

A great way to start is to begin utilizing those empty drawers and cabinets and fill them up with relevant things. These cabinets were designed to look good and be practical. The latter seems to be missing in most cases and that needs to change.

While storage does get half the job done, the other half of the equation requires you to start changing your habits of bringing unnecessary things to your house. Start by jotting down a list of things before you go out to shop. Things that are absolutely essential are what you are aiming for. Start training yourself to avoid giving in to temptations. You might see a new snack or a practical looking desk lamp, but these things would not necessarily be classified as essential. Stop, turn around, and leave the aisle. Focus on the essentials only. Stick to the basics and do yourself a favor by organizing the spaces in your house.

Minimalism is a lifestyle. It is not just limited to the way you store things, declutter them, and stick to the essentials. It also encircles your living, eating, working habits, along with relationships. All you need is an inspiration to begin with, a guide to help you get there, and a sense of realization when you start achieving the milestones you have set for yourself.

You can draw quite a lot of inspiration by browsing the internet. Pick out your top 10 images of a minimalist home and start jotting down ideas. They have served hundreds of people with innovative and creative ideas. They certainly helped me out when I was starting out with my minimalist lifestyle.

Having a source of inspiration gives us much-needed direction and allows us to fully take in the minimalist lifestyle. It further clarifies our eventual goal as well. Who knows, you might come across a picture that you model your home after.

The Takeaway

In this chapter, we learned:

- Minimalism is more than just decluttering, it is about picturing how you want your home to look.
- Good habits take time to develop, it will take a while to stop the habit of bringing home unnecessary items.
- Storage is an important aspect of minimalism, but don't forget to actually remove things from your home, don't just find clever ways to keep storing things.
- Stick to basics, forget the luxuries, only keep what you absolutely need. The fancier the things are in your home, the more difficult it will be for you to eventually free yourself of them.
- Remember the one in, one out rule. If you bring home something, you have to remove another.
- The internet is a good source to seek inspiration if you are struggling to picture your minimalistic home. Images help us visualize our own scenario and goals.

Coming up next, we will be looking at a part of the home that literally provides us with everything our body needs; the kitchen!

8

THE KITCHEN

> *"It is always the simple that produces the marvelous."*
>
> AMELIA BARR

Not too long ago, every time I visited my kitchen it reminded me of a popular show called "Kitchen Nightmares", where a renowned chef named Gordon Ramsay would quite literally take the entire kitchen apart to expose how dirty it was and how that affected the food quality. You might be wondering why that is.

My kitchen was a nightmare. Don't get me wrong, it was sparkling clean. The issue was the heap of clutter that I had piled up in my kitchen. I could never find what I was looking for when I needed it. This became quite a bit of a problem and I managed to cook a few too many dishes as well.

Naturally, I decided to take things out and place them where I could reach them more easily. Before I knew it, I had almost everything laid out on the counter and the entire exercise brought me back to square one.

In this chapter, we are going to take a look at what you can do to make your kitchen the minimalistic haven you want while also keeping it functional.

Sort through your cupboards

My kitchen was full of outdated, expired cans, lying around for no reason at all. Old pots were gathering dust and rust while I continued to use only a select few. Sound familiar?

The fact of the matter is that quite a lot of us tend to do this. In the years after I discovered the eternal freedom that minimalism is, I have helped out quite a few people with their homes, and every single kitchen I visited had the same problem; clutter upon clutter.

Start asking yourself some hard questions about the items you have in your cabinets. Do you really need all of them? Are those pots that you bought and last used years ago doing any good? When was the last time you made a sandwich using the panini press?

How about the drawers?

Keep asking yourself how badly you really need every item in your kitchen the next time you are in your kitchen and start piling up things on one side whenever you realize that an item does you no good. Let's shift our attention away from the cabinets now and focus on the drawers instead. Old tea towels, over 21 different knives, when I only used two of them at most. Clear up space in your drawers and you will be able to use it for other purposes.

These days many of us live in apartments with smaller kitchens. There isn't an inch of space to waste and you could probably use all the extra room you can get. Instead of buying extra shelves to clear your drawers of utensils and other items, clear up the space you already have by decluttering the surplus of items that are serving no purpose.

Trust me, the food will still taste great. That is never going to change. What will change though is the way your kitchen will begin to look and feel. Everything can now be rearranged and organized.

Rule of thumb: if you aren't going to use it, either don't buy it or bin it if you already have. 21 knives? I was surely not thinking straight when I decided to go and buy those. Now, my kitchen has just two knives and my partner and I continue to cook good and healthy food, no worries. It now feels like the others were never there to begin with.

Don't Forget The Counters!

Counters are meant to be used for a specific purpose. If there is anything on top of the counter that shouldn't belong there, get rid of it or put it back where it belongs. Start training your brain to put things where they are supposed to be. You will learn how good of a habit this is and how you will eventually know exactly where to look if you are trying to find something specific. Right now, you might have to turn the entire place upside down to find something you might have not seen in years. Avoid falling for that trap. Plan ahead and plan well.

A clear counter in an organized and well-maintained kitchen promotes healthy eating in ways you cannot imagine. The kitchen itself will feel like an appealing place to be in making it more conducive to cooking and resulting in fewer takeout meals, saving you money. I know I would never eat anything out of a kitchen that is cluttered and smelling of odors other than that of fresh food and vegetables.

It also greatly helps to reduce the number of plates, trays, and other such items if you only have a small family living within your walls. You aren't expecting the entire neighborhood to show up for dinner at your place, why keep that many plates then?

Think about every single cent that you invest in the kitchen from here on out. Make it your top priority that the only things to enter the house, apart from the family, are the absolute essentials. This will serve you equally well and will help you greatly reduce the amount of clutter.

It's not clutter if you use it

Remember that being a minimalist does not mean getting rid of everything indiscriminately. If you had a big dinner and there are quite a bit of leftovers, store them. Don't throw away food unless it has gone bad. Use your freezer to preserve your food and consume it wisely. It also helps to start cooking proportionately. There is no point in cooking five bowls of rice when there are only two of you dining.

Stop wasting both space and food and start utilizing everything. Mark your calendar and continue to develop these habits for the next 30 days. After a month, you will realize just how incredible you feel, how organized things are, and how easy things will become for you. The kitchen is one of the busiest rooms in the home, it makes sense to keep it as ordered as possible.

The Takeaway

This chapter focused primarily on the kitchen. We also learned that:

- The kitchen can easily become cluttered with items that we thought we would need, but when was the last time you actually used the panini press, or the pasta maker?
- Don't sacrifice space so you can keep some old pots. They are just gathering dust in your cupboard and are better off going to a larger family that will make use of it.
- The better you organize things, the more space you will discover you have in your kitchen. Organize your drawers and don't have several different kinds of knives in there when you only need two.
- Train your brain to always put things back

where they belong. Keep the counters clear and your kitchen will look a lot more inviting.

- Minimalism is about using things wisely, not just removing clutter. Use things well and you will still be living a minimalist lifestyle. Cook with portions in mind, for example, and store leftovers for another day instead of throwing them out.
- Be sure to notice the difference 30 days from your kitchen revolution.

In the next chapter, we will visit the living room and really bring the place to life through small tweaks.

9

THE LIVING ROOM

"Truth is ever to be found in simplicity, and not in the multiplicity and confusion of things."

ISAAC NEWTON

The living room – a place where we forget the worries of the world, sit back, relax and enjoy our favorite TV shows. This is where we normally find ourselves the most comfortable. Naturally, for a place this important, it must look and feel equally good. However, lately, I have noticed that people try to seek out perfection that just never seems to exist. They get inspired by all the right things but end up doing the polar opposite.

Living rooms are one of the primary rooms of the house and it makes every bit of sense to make them look appealing to us and to anyone who may visit our home. An elegant seven-seater, a fancy coffee table, a contemporary yet stylish lamp in the corner to brighten up the place. The massive gallery or window that lights up the place evenly and allows the space to be prominent. It all seems nice but we still end up spoiling the perfect setting with too many things.

Less is More!

For the sake of discussion, let us assume we are facing two rooms. Both rooms are equal in dimensions and both have equal features such as large windows, chimney, floor carpet, lights, etc. The one on the left is brimming with exquisite and tasteful furniture, designed to look like something from the Victorian era. The room is lit with yellow warm lights, and the window looks out into the front of the house. It sounds nice, right?

The room on the right has natural light that flows through the windows, ample to light up the almost vacant room that comprises only one L-shaped couch, a small coffee table sitting on a piece of rug that matches the color scheme. While the room has less in it, the ambiance is brought to life by the space. It feels bigger and roomier, and it certainly is more pleasant on the eyes.

The simple difference between the two is the approach. One show-cases elegance, the other provides a more inviting feel. It makes everything look a lot more open. All you really need can be achieved with a lot less and it will still offer you a lot more than the former option.

Clear your space

What do you really need? A comfortable sofa, a little chest of drawers to keep my DVDs and books in, an elegant coffee table, and a plant in the corner to bring freshness and life. After doing the necessary decluttering, you will be thrilled to see how elegant your sitting room now looks and feels. Lastly, the sheer amount of space and light work together in perfect harmony to promote a breathable and enjoyable setting. Why wouldn't anyone want to be there?

Sofas

Of course, the big things are easy to clear. Perhaps you had a 7-seater couch when the kids were at home, but they have since gone to university and you can reduce the amount of seating. Perhaps you only need a couple of armchairs. Once you have removed your old sofa and installed a couple of tasteful armchairs you will definitely see an immediate difference.

Furniture

Perhaps you are one of those people who has a large wall cabinet with glass shelves that are home to all sorts of knick-knacks, souvenirs and mementos from trips abroad, special events, etc. Make this part of your list of things to discard. Yes, all those items will have special significance for you, but you can't hold onto them forever. There comes a time when you need to realize that the happy memories will live on within you, you do not need a tacky sombrero souvenir from the airport to remind you of your vacation in Mexico.

Once you have removed enough of the souvenirs you can think about letting go of that large and bulky wall cabinet that takes up so much room and doesn't allow natural light to illuminate your sitting room.

The small items

Once you have cleared up space, the real challenge awaits. Small items such as DVDs, magazines, mail and so on, tend to pile up and we easily overlook these. They can really stand in the way of our ideal settings. I faced a similar situation as well, and quite a few times I almost fell for the obvious trap. Instead of buying and installing bookshelves on the wall and storing books and magazines, I decided to change my habits and you can do the same.

Magazines

If you buy a magazine, ensure that you read it within a week and then get rid of it. Keep no place for magazines to stick around because if they are there for longer than they need to be, it will be more difficult to throw them out later on.

Stop procrastinating

Avoid delaying things. If you are done reading your mail, magazines, and newspapers, have them taken out and sent for recycling. For important mail or clippings, you can always maintain a ring folder and store it in a drawer or a cabinet. Or use the digitizing tip from earlier and take a picture with your smartphone.

Put things back in their place

Perhaps you're an avid music listener. Always ensure that any CD remains in a specific place and not on the table or on the TV stand. Organize yourself and ensure that things are always put back in their place. Not only does this habit ensure you keep your prized possessions safe, but it also saves them from being trampled upon by kids or pets.

Tidy up the cables

One of the biggest bugbears we have is the amount of cabling that our devices require. These items that give us so much joy also create a lot of mess with their cables. Our phones, tablets and laptops come with a bundle of cables, but so do our games consoles, DVD players, cable TV systems, surround sound systems, etc.

Invest in small cable tidies, wire binders or wiring solutions to hide excess and exposed wires. Having a cluster of wires will spoil the beauty and serenity of the living room and would also cause trouble for you when you need to dive in to find the right wire which connects the Xbox to your TV, for example.

. . .

YOUR LIVING ROOM is a place where you can unwind and relax a little. Do not make it a habit of leaving stuff around. Whether you come home from school, the office or from running errands, put things where they are supposed to be before entering the living room for a bit of a break. Piling things up will eventually convert into a habit and you will go back to creating clutter. That is counter-productive and must be avoided at all costs.

These simple tweaks won't cost you much and can be quickly achieved. Have a good look around your living room and start taking action. Try and remove things that shouldn't be anywhere near the living room. Before you know it, your living room will change from a dreary place to this incredible space of genuine comfort and pleasure.

The Takeaway

Time for another quick recap:

- Less is definitely more when it comes to minimalism. A crowded living room will be less pleasant than a sparse one.
- Try to cut back on large and bulky items that can rob your living room of much needed space and light. A larger sofa than is necessary can be a bonus when you have people over, but all you might need is a few armchairs that take up less space.
- Get rid of the knick-knacks and you can also

get rid of that massive wall cabinet that holds them. That will definitely free up lots of space.

- Small items can often be more difficult to organize than larger ones. Be sure to put them all back where they belong after using them. Things being out of place can easily clutter your living room.

- Get rid of things on a regular basis. Once you have read a magazine, take it to your dentist's for the waiting room. Simple tweaks like this can truly change a lot of things

IN THE NEXT CHAPTER, we will now be shifting our focus to our bedroom and looking at how minimalism can help us find flaws in our bedroom and how certain things can affect a good night's sleep.

10

THE BEDROOM

"Purity and simplicity are the two wings with which man soars above the earth and all temporary nature."

THOMAS KEMPIS

The bedroom is a place that is supposed to be comfortable, clean, cozy, and quiet. It is where we get our sleep, it is where we wake up and get dressed. This is where most of our days begin and end. Needless to say, if you take away the comforts, this just becomes a room with a bed in it. There are many things that can be considered a comfort, but are actually clutter. While it makes no sense to crowd our bedroom with non-essentials, sometimes it is the essentials themselves that cause disturbances and nuisance. How?

Imagine a small, cozy-looking bedroom. Everything seems perfect, except that the bedsheet is all messed up, as if someone got out in a hurry and left it. To the side of the bed are a pair of shoes while on the other side there is a paper bag or two from your favorite outlet. This ruins the overall look and feel of the bedroom, but there are habits you can adopt to ensure that doesn't happen.

Make the bed

It sounds simple and perhaps a little trivial, but making the bed is a basic habit that is easy to adopt and takes about five seconds each morning. We normally get up, have our shower and head straight out of the bedroom. Just add one little step to your routine before leaving the bedroom: ensure you make the bed properly. Leaving the sheets in a mess does not really give us a warm and cozy feeling when we come back home after a long day and try to get some sleep. Making your bed before you leave will ensure that the bed is ready for you every time you return home.

Keep shoes out of the bedroom

Secondly, leaving your shoes or slippers next to the bed isn't exactly a healthy habit either. You might have walked from a dirty area and this would only bring that dirt, mud, and sand into your bedroom. Always leave these outside or next to the door. Buy a shoe rack if you need to, but ensure that your shoes do not enter the home after being outside.

Tidy away any bags

Imagine you have come home with a little clothes shopping and left the bags by the bed to be put away later. Your partner or your kids do the same, placing them next to yours. Pretty soon you will find yourself with less space to move into your bedroom. Instead, make the effort to put your purchases away to maintain a sense of order and harmony in the bedroom. You can find a bigger bag to pack the other smaller ones.

Make the bedroom a toy-free zone

If you have children, it is perhaps understood that they will be seen playing with toys in your bedroom. There are times when parents need to enforce some ground rules for their children. If your children play around with their toys in your bedroom, at least establish a rule that they should take their toys with them when they leave. You could create a little play zone for the kids where they can have all their fun.

Power down your electronics

It is advisable that you reduce the number of electronic items in your room. A study that was conducted showed that having fewer electronic items in the bedroom allows us to sleep much better than a room that has more of them. Of course, you need your cell phone, your laptop, your TV, and so on, however, you can switch these off and place them in another room while you sleep.

Keep it clean

Keep your bedroom clean and always ensure that you and your partner never leave dirty clothes lying around the bedroom. The best practice is to change your habit of delaying matters. Act quickly and act now. If you have to do laundry, get it done. Once the clothes are washed, fold them, and store them in their designated place. You can hang the ones which you know you will wear the next morning. This saves time and energy if you need to rush and would allow you to get ready far more quickly.

A simple and elegant bedroom always sounds and feels inviting. It is where you truly gather your thoughts and go to sleep to wake up refreshed, recharged, and ready to go. A messy bedroom would only push negativity your way. You will neither be able to sleep properly nor enjoy the tranquility and serene comfort of the room itself.

The Takeaway

We have learned that simple tweaks and changes can greatly impact our lives. In the case of the bedroom, we learned that:

- Bedrooms should be clean and tidy if you want them to be comfortable.
- Adopt the habit of always making your bed in

the morning so each evening you return to a
tidy and inviting environment.

- Never let things pile up in the bedroom, it
  doesn't take long to tidy away clean clothes, or
  put away any new purchases.
- Shoes should stay out of the bedroom so you do
  not track dirt into an area that should be all
  about rest and relaxation.
- Laundry, if there is any, should be done as soon
  as possible so a pile of it does not accumulate.
- Make a rule about your children leaving their
  toys in the bedroom. When they leave, the toys
  go with them.
- Be sure to switch off any electrical items when
  you are sleeping. Better yet, move them to
  another room to improve your sleep.

In the next chapter, we will now be turning to the place
which has served major companies as a starting point; the
garage.

11

THE GARAGE AND/OR SHED

"Simplicity is making the journey of this life with just baggage enough."

CHARLES DUDLEY WARNER

Ah, the garage. A place where for some odd reason our creativity hits a new high. This part of the house has pushed countless people to become a success story. If you are surprised to hear this, take a breath before I unveil who turned out to be a leading example that started in a garage and now has become one of the most successful companies in the world: Apple.

To quite a lot of us, the garage is a place that offers ample space for us to park our car, and still have room to carry out repairs and mend a few things. The iconic board where we hang our tools, the vacuum cleaner that sits in the corner, old boxes of newspapers, magazines, children's toys, the rack with our spare wheels, there is just so much to be found here. However, being a minimalist, I will pose you the same question yet again. Do we really need all of that to stick around? Can we not clear the clutter and create more space? Sure we can, and we will!

Why the garage matters

You may be wondering why I have devoted a chapter to the garage. "Surely if there was ever a place in the house that could be used as a dumping ground for odds and ends, it is the garage," you may be thinking. The reason is that garages hold a lot of potentials and are genuinely a place where we can do so much. There are tons of videos where people have used their garages for their science projects, mechanical tasks, and so much more. It then makes sense to ensure that our garage is always spacious enough to house what we need and serve as a place where we can put things which we may later discard, sell, or give away to others.

However, not everyone is going to use their garage to start the next Microsoft or Apple. For many of us, the garage is about having storage space. Throughout the entire process of decluttering, you cannot expect to remove a large number of items, box them, and have them collected or donated to others all within the same day. While the process is underway, you will need a place where you can keep these boxes. What better place than the safe and secure garage which has the space that your house may not. This, however, is only possible if your garage is not already cluttered with things like your old bicycle that you have not ridden in years. Clear these out first to make room for other items to come.

Clear Out the Rest!

Now comes the tricky part. Clearing out the garage is almost as difficult to do as decluttering the rest of your home. It takes time and energy, but then again, that is to be expected when clearing up clutter. If you have committed to adopting a new lifestyle, expect quite a few radical changes to come your way before you are truly able to enjoy it.

Old projects

Begin by taking care of that old project you started working on years ago. Let us be very honest and accept the fact that you aren't likely to work on it, and from the looks of it, it will remain the same way for years to come if you don't get rid of it. It is time to say goodbye to your unfinished project and be done with it. Keeping it around will only add to the clutter we are trying to remove.

Long term occupants

Most garages are home to things like empty tins and old flower pots that have been hanging around for ages with no purpose. Now is the time to take some action. We stored them; now we decide whether we use them or show them the door. For tins, it's a straight ticket to the recycle bin. For the flower pots, you can either pick these up and fill it with soil and seeds or add it to the list of things you are about to discard. There is no reason to delay matters here; decide now and then stick to your decision.

If you find anything else in the garage that you haven't used for a very long time, even if it is a vehicle, sell it and earn some money. You can get in touch with scrap yards or dealers to have the vehicle removed and taken care of for you. You would be doing yourself a favor by clearing out such a huge space. Now, you can have more room to carry out other operations more easily.

Clean, clean, clean

Give your garage a thorough cleaning. Clean up those oil drips and slicks. Use washing agents to help you take care of tire marks, oil splatter and paint that may have dripped on the floor. The objective is to ensure we have a clean looking garage that is brightly lit and allows us to use the space without any clutter.

There are so many inspiring ideas for how you can put your garage to good use once it is empty of clutter. You can use it to make your own beer, turn it into a workshop. Use it to learn a new skill, such as pottery or woodworking. Or you could even get some friends around and start a band. The possibilities are almost endless.

The Takeaway

Garages are endlessly useful spaces. To successfully apply the minimalist principles we should:

- Understand that the garage holds a lot of potentials and should not be considered an easy dumping ground for anything that won't fit in the home.
- However, the garage can be used to temporarily store items that are waiting to be donated to goodwill, or taken to be recycled, or sold.
- Before you can use it as temporary storage, you need to clear out any clutter that is already taking up space.
- Many garages have long term occupants, such as old DIY projects, or various tins and flower pots that have been waiting for their time to become useful. Be honest about how likely it is that this time will come, and then discard these items.
- Clean the garage floor and walls thoroughly to make it as comfortable as possible.
- Keep it well-lit and you now have a great space to use as extra storage, or for something more pleasant.

In the next chapter, we will take a quick tour of the bathroom and see how minimalism can help us declutter this part of the house.

12

THE BATHROOM

"Simple pleasures are the last healthy refuge in a complex world."

OSCAR WILDE

"Did you know that there is an essential room in your house that we always tend to overlook?"

I posed this question to quite a lot of the people I have helped over the years. The response has always been a "Huh?" or "What are you talking about?". I don't blame them for responding this way. It is due to the fact that this specific space, despite being so essential, is overlooked and dismissed by quite a lot of us when it comes to minimalism.

I am referring to the bathroom. It is an essential room that is most commonly used without much thought. It is where we go through our daily ablutions and prepare ourselves to face the outside world. It is also where we come to relax after a long day, perhaps for a soak in the bathtub, or a relaxing hot shower that will wash away the day. It is rarely a place that we consider in terms of how we can simplify it and make it less cluttered, but this is exactly what I am proposing with this chapter.

Decor

This may seem like an unusual thing to consider in the bathroom, but your bathroom decor can have a big impact on how cluttered it may feel, especially if your bathroom isn't particularly spacious. Most houses will have tiled walls, some will be painted, some may even have wallpaper. However the walls are decorated it is always helpful if the pattern is as neutral as possible and doesn't seem "busy".

Why is this important? Well, the bathroom is one of the only places in the home that engages all the senses. The sounds of the water. The fragrances of the various soaps, shampoos, gels and lotions. The tactile feel of water, or other substances on your skin, the pruning of your skin when you have been in the water. With all your senses being on high alert you are subconsciously more aware of your surroundings. A cluttered feel to the decor can have an impact on how well you are able to relax in your bathroom.

I'm not saying you need to repaint the walls, or retile the entire bathroom, but consider replacing your patterned shower curtain with a plain one that is more gentle on your eyes. If you have a radio in the bathroom it may help to give you a boost in the morning, but in the evening when you want to relax having it on can be more of a nuisance. So try leaving it turned off and see if you leave the bathroom feeling more relaxed.

Lotions & Potions

I mentioned the various soaps, shampoos, gels, and lotions earlier. You don't even need to take a look into your bathroom to know what I am saying is true. Just picture your bathroom in your mind's eye and you will understand what I mean when I write that most of us have far more when it comes to creams, lotions, and soaps than we actually need. Many of us are presented with gift boxes during the festive season, the trouble is that we end up with a stockpile to get through.

Try regifting some of these gift boxes. It might seem ungrateful, but your quality of life is the most important thing and it is in your interest to live a life that is free of clutter. Not all gifts constitute clutter and if you genuinely believe that you will use the various soaps and gels you have received, then it makes sense to find a storage space and work your way through them. But consider regifting the ones that you don't think you will use as someone else may benefit from them and it would clear more space in your bathroom.

Waste

The bathroom is often a place where shelves become crammed with empty plastic bottles. Tiny slivers of soap bars that are too small to be used can clog the drain. Meanwhile the trash can may be overflowing with cotton pads used to remove makeup. These all have an impact on your experience in the bathroom and do not make for a very relaxing, minimalist lifestyle. The answer? Be sure to take action and do not let waste accumulate. Be assiduous about emptying out the trash can in the bathroom and clearing the empty bottles of product. As for the slivers of soap, unclog that drain and get rid of them.

Towels

For most of us the bathroom is one of the smaller rooms in the home. Yet many of us insist on keeping our various towels in there. Face towels, hand towels, bath sheets. If you are running out of space in the bathroom the answer is not to add another cupboard, or some more shelves. See if you can cut back on the things you are keeping in there. Could the towels go elsewhere? Maybe you could take the towel you need when you go into the bathroom rather than having them all there together.

The Takeaway

Let us look at what we learned:

- Bathrooms can have a big impact on how we start and end each day. It is best if they can be as pleasant, comfortable and relaxing as possible.
- Since bathrooms have the potential to engage all the senses it makes sense to adjust your decor so the room doesn't appear too "busy" and cluttered. Go for neutral colors and plain shower curtains that are easier on the eyes.
- Don't overstock on soaps, shampoos and shower gels as they will clutter the bathroom. If you are gifted a lot of soaps over the festive season, try regifting to remove them from your home.
- Act quickly and often to remove empty plastic bottles, tiny slivers of leftover soap, and empty overflowing trash cans to make your bathroom an oasis of calm.
- All you towels do not need to be kept in the bathroom, they can be stored elsewhere, just remember to take a towel with you when you go for a shower or take a bath.

In the next chapter, we will revisit a few concepts and also look at good habits you can adopt to further enhance your experience as a minimalist.

13

TOP MINIMALIST HABITS THAT APPLY TO ANY HOME

"Simplicity is the glory of expression."

WALT WHITMAN

Practically speaking, you now have all the basic know-how about what minimalism is and how you can start to declutter your home and set it free. We have learned again and again that having more space allows us to do a lot more. We can free up space by clearing out any excess, and using items that have been gathering dust all this time to give the home a more vibrant look and feel. We can donate items we don't use and contribute back to society and feel good about the act as well.

Taking the Next Step

While all of this seems good and promising, there are a few things you should start doing to further enhance the minimalist experience and truly adopt a lifestyle that is going to do wonders for you in the future. A year from now, you will be a completely different person, living life to its fullest and never feeling shallow or unaccomplished again. Your relationships will improve and so will your health. It is a win-win situation. So, what exactly are these things that you can do to amplify the effects? Let us have a look.

CLEANLINESS IS THE KEY – Cleanliness is the key to invite positivity into your life, your body, and your home. Make it a habit to clean as you go. Stop delaying matters thinking that you can sort this out later. There is a good chance that when this 'later' scenario arrives, you may already have other tasks to complete and you would end up pushing this simple task further back.

DISHES; do them after you use them – After a pleasant meal with your family, promote the habit of cleaning the dishes immediately. Do not let them sit on the counter. This will give way to unpleasant odors and bacteria. Clean the dishes as soon as you are done eating.

. . .

You've Got Mail! – Sort through your mail as soon as you receive it. If it helps, make two piles on the table. Put the important mail in one pile while the rest go in the other. Have the not-so-important ones sent out to the recycle bin and keep the ones you need to reference later on.

Clear the countertops before you call it a night – Quite self-explanatory. Make it a habit to tidy up the kitchen counters after you use them. As an added measure, give them a quick clean before you turn in for the night.

Only buy what you need – This might need some time to truly develop as a habit but make some strict rules about what enters your home and what doesn't. Whenever you or your partner go out to the store, only buy things that are needed. Anything else is just a waste of money. Trust me; you will be thankful you developed this habit when you see your savings increase.

Keep an eye on the little spaces – If you stop paying attention to these little nooks and crannies around the house, they may start to build clutter. Eventually, you will be back where you started. Ensure that you clean these and declutter them often.

.   .   .

DECLUTTERING ISN'T A ONE-TIME PROCESS – Decluttering is a never-ending process that you will need to carry out on a regular basis. Stay on top of decluttering so you can ensure your house and your health remains in pristine condition.

JOT DOWN SYSTEMS AND PROCESSES – Create systems and processes which help you know what needs to be done when mail arrives, what needs to be done when you wake up, what needs to be done before bed...etc. Once you get into the loop and start repeating the same processes over and over again, you will soon implement the system of keeping your house free from clutter and sticking to the basics, which will automatically help elevate the living standards of your family.

YOU HAVE EVERYTHING YOU NEED – Learn how to be satisfied with all that you have. There is no reason why you should feel like you want more of this and more of that. Minimalism allows you to always feel fulfilled with the essentials that you need and have.

ENJOY THE SPACE you have created – Creating space doesn't always mean you should then use them for other purposes. Sometimes, you just need space to be there to make things a lot roomier.

. . .

LEARN HOW TO SAY NO – Birthdays, anniversaries, or other special days, are times when you expect people to send gifts your way. It is probably wise to get used to saying "No, thank you!" to stop possible clutter coming your way. Make it a habit to encourage people to do something practical on your birthday like donate to your favorite charity.

QUALITY OVER QUANTITY – The objective behind minimalism is to aim for quality. This applies equally to the items you end up purchasing. If you can, buy fewer items of good quality as opposed to more items of poorer quality.

REUSE, repurpose, resell – Flowerpots? Reuse them. The loft space? Repurpose it and use it again for a better purpose. Old vehicles, magazines, and toys? Resell them, if you can. Learn how to apply this motto to everything you own. Who knows, you might find better alternative uses for some items you own.

KEEP INSPIRING YOURSELF – The quest to perfection never ends, and it doesn't with your sources of inspiration either. Continue browsing the internet to seek out more sources of inspiration. Learn from success stories and find out what made them such a success.

The Takeaway

In this chapter, we learned:

- Cleanliness is next to Godliness, apparently. In any case, keeping your home clean is a good habit to have.
- Don't let the dirty dishes pile up in the sink, just get them done. Also, clear the kitchen counters of clutter while you are at it.
- Sort through your mail as soon as possible so it doesn't pile up.
- Visit the store with a list of things you need and stick to the list, don't be tempted to buy other things that you don't need.
- Remember that decluttering is not a one-off event, you need to keep an eye so areas do not become cluttered once more, especially the smaller nooks and crannies.
- Make a note of any systems that can help you to keep on top of things.
- Learn to be satisfied with what you have. There is no reason to feel that you are missing anything. Instead, enjoy the space you have freed up.
- You can find a polite way to refuse a gift if you think it will cause clutter in your home. Otherwise think about regifting it to someone else.
- If you do need to buy things, go for quality. The

item will last longer and you'll need fewer of them, so less clutter.

- Learn to see clutter in a different light. Items that were previously useless can be used in a different way for a new purpose you hadn't previously considered. Don't forget about reselling items too.

In the next chapter, we will talk about the most feared aspect about minimalism - going back into old habits. I know this happens to quite a few of us, which is why it is essential to know how to avoid this from happening.

14

SLIPPING BACK INTO OLD HABITS

"You have succeeded in life when all you really want is only what you really need."

VERNON HOWARD

While we near the end of the book, we cannot overlook one key aspect that has taken quite a lot of minimalists back to square one. It is something that we cannot truly control in a specific way. However, it is not impossible to avoid this from happening and avoid slipping back into old habits.

Old habits are always a part of us and there may always be an unconscious temptation to do what comes easiest, which would mean slipping back into a bad habit. Maybe your bad habit is that you leave the shopping on the kitchen counter when you get back home and neglect to put it away, leaving it all pile up. Maybe another bad habit is only doing laundry when you are about to run out of clothes, letting dirty clothes pile up and overflow in the laundry hamper. Slipping back into old habits is a possibility. I am not saying this to create a sense of unease, but I am here to warn you that it is easy for people to end up back where they started. Try to visualize the kind of lifestyle you want for yourself. Yes, you want a minimalist lifestyle, but what does this mean for you? What are the habits that you want to change and how do you think that will improve your life? Grab your pen and paper and make a list.

Once you have your list, think about the process that you will have to go through to make the changes work for you in the long run. Once you feel that you have successfully adopted your new habits, start thinking about how you can move on to other changes to further enhance your life. Beware, while we can do the old trick of telling our brain that there is no going back into old habits now, it doesn't always work. It all comes down to your willpower. The stronger it is, the harder it is for old habits to reappear.

Yes, minimalism changes you as a person. It reforms the way you think, the way you behave, and adds an element of mindfulness. However, this doesn't guarantee you that your changed persona will remain as it is. There is a good chance that you might still fall for old habits if you are not careful enough.

Some Quick Tips

Here are some quick tips that you can use to ensure the above doesn't happen to you:

1. Be extremely mindful of the sudden urges you might encounter along the way. Shrug them off right away!
2. If you spot even a hint of an old habit creeping its way back in, take evasive action.
3. Think every decision through to its end. There are times we might make bad decisions, which would essentially lead us back to square one.
4. Beware of people who question your new lifestyle. They may encourage you to go back to your old habits.

With that said, you are now fully equipped to pursue your own venture into the world of minimalism. Where you go from this point on is up to you.

AFTERWORD

The journey into the world of minimalism is filled with achievements and challenges alike. There is no shortcut to becoming a minimalist. Each and every one of us has a unique set of priorities, a different lifestyle, and quite a few other elements to consider. Claiming that there is a "one size fits all" kind of a deal here is just wrong.

Minimalism is a concept that has improved a massive number of lives. Decluttering is what plays a vital role, and it is not just limited to that excess, space-consuming pile of objects lying around in the house, it goes far beyond that. Physical and mental decluttering, when combined, allow us to truly seek out minimalism.

I personally wish to thank each of my readers who picked up a copy of this book and placed their trust in me to explore the world of minimalism. Your trust is what drove me to write this book in the first place. I truly feel that this concept can help change lives for the better. For years, I have helped people undergo this transformation but it always felt like I could do more. It eventually dawned upon me that writing a book would allow me to spread my knowledge to a bigger audience, and today, you are holding every bit of that knowledge in your hands. That, for me, is quite an achievement.

We started with almost no knowledge about what minimalism was. We went through chapter by chapter and started to understand that minimalism wasn't just about throwing stuff away. It is a lifestyle that shows us that we can live an equally if not more fascinating and fulfilling life by sticking to the essentials. We learned how to differentiate between what we want and what we need.

We then moved on to some practical tips and tricks to start revamping your house, decluttering the garage, the bedroom, the bathroom, and using the newly found space in one way or another. Sure, there are little warning signs that say "Turn around!" but we learned how to move past that. Falling for old habits is what we are to avoid at all costs.

Now that you have a wealth of knowledge, it is time to embark on your own journey. Use this book whenever you feel like you need ideas and apply them to your life. See how it changes things for you and what results it brings. There is no point in reading this book and then keeping it on a shelf with the others without ever applying the newly gained knowledge.

How you proceed from this point on will determine where you will be in the next few years. If you are truly passionate about changing your lifestyle for the better, act today! The more you delay matters, the more you are pushing a new and improved life further beyond reach. The going will get tough, but remember, you have everything you need to emerge as a winner.

Always continue reading great books and seek great inspiration from material online. You can always grab a copy of my other books "Minimalist" and "Declutter," and I will soon be publishing "Decluttering your Home" in order for all of you to gain even greater insight and knowledge.

Lastly, we all have this great ability to be self-disciplined and go deeper into minimalism. The key is to get our minds out of trouble and keep it that way.

REFERENCES

Becker, J. (2018). The Minimalist Home. Goodreads Author

Layne, E. (2019). The Minimalist Way. Althea Press

Vidiella, A. S. (2014). 150 Best Minimalist House Ideas. Harper Design

UNSTUFF YOUR HOME

SIMPLE HOUSE CLEANING HACKS TO
DECLUTTER AND TIDY UP YOUR HOME,
LET GO OF UNUSED THINGS, ORGANIZE
YOUR ROOMS, AND ACHIEVE FREEDOM
ONCE AND FOR ALL

INTRODUCTION

Everyone gathers possessions in one form or another. Depending on how you accumulate possessions in your life, it can create clutter in your home that may be significantly more than that of other individuals. Handling clutter can be a challenge if you don't know the right steps to take.

The clutter in your home may be in the form of clothes, shoes, toys, dinnerware sets, and so on. As you pile up these items without discarding, you slowly create clutter in your home.

Since you may struggle to deal with clutter in the home, I'm confident that this book will provide a solution to your problem. The answer it offers includes vital information on how to stop yourself from accumulating clutter and how to eliminate existing clutter in the home through decluttering.

Solutions such as learning to say no to gifts, decluttering public and private spaces in the home, and maintaining the habits you develop are all introduced. If you are in doubt about my ability to help you, then let me tell you a little about myself.

I am a 37-year old mother of two kids who used to be in a similar predicament. I was working for a magazine company and used to struggle with clutter before I eventually quit the job.

During my time at the company, there were days I had to take some of my work home, to meet deadlines. Despite this action, I was usually unable to do much at home. Why?

You guessed it; in great part, it was due to the presence of clutter in my home. This created distractions that made it difficult for me to focus on my work. I was working hard, but inefficiently. Books and magazines were stacked all around me. Laundry piled up. The flow of the furniture just didn't work. I couldn't really get anything done with all of the "junk" around me.

To overcome this problem, I started researching ways to get rid of clutter. Through my research, I learned a lot about decluttering. As the name implies, it is the process of getting rid of clutter.

After engaging in the decluttering process around my home, I noticed changes in my life. It improved my concentration and efficiency while working. Also, I learned to be content. Through contentment, I was able to avoid falling into the trap of accumulation, which would have caused me to create more clutter.

By going through this book, you'll learn many things. When you apply the tips and information in this book, benefits accrue to you. Things you will learn include:

- Why you accumulate "stuff"
- Understanding hoarding, its effects, and symptoms
- Learning about minimalism and Danshari
- Applying Danshari to your life
- Unstuff your home
- Keeping up your new habits

As you learn about these areas and apply them to your life, you will quickly start noticing changes. Before that, you must understand that you need to put in the time and effort to make these changes. Decluttering, as a process, takes a lot of time to complete.

Regardless, it is a process that grants you small wins that pile up. This means that you get the opportunity to apply the decluttering process to a small section of your home, like your bedroom, and then compare it with other parts. This will give you the motivation you need to complete the process.

When you apply everything you learn in this book, an example of the change you experience is an increase in the amount of money available to you. This is because you no longer buy things you don't need.

Eliminating clutter in the home can also make it possible for you to live in a smaller, less expensive apartment or home. Let me explain. I've had the opportunity to work with other individuals to help get rid of their clutter problems. Some of these individuals are those who continuously hoard things. These individuals have also learned to overcome this problem and engage in the decluttering process. As a result, they were able to move from a large apartment to a smaller, more economical and efficient space.

I am confident that this book will change your life through the information it contains. The information herein is tailored to address the various issues relating to clutter. These include the causes and effects.

Dealing with clutter is one thing you must do swiftly. Delaying this action will only further complicate your situation as it leads to a drop in your productivity, and can also affect your relationship with others. If you're struggling with hoarding, then you have no time to waste. Hoarding harms both your health and your home environment. Most of us think of the extremes of hoarding, based on what we've seen on television, for example. But hoarding isn't necessarily harmful only under those extremes. Do you:

- Buy excessive food at the grocery store?
- Have duplicates of many items in your home?
- Feel uncomfortable purging yourself of unused items?
- Have a lot of piles around the house?

These are signs of a more minor habit of hoarding, and it can be a real burden when it comes to how you live your life, and how you can fulfill your potential. Excess stuff doesn't just clutter your home; it clutters your mind and heart.

If you want to overcome these issues, then you must start now. As I said, decluttering is a process that takes time.

Therefore, you can't waste any more time dragging your feet.

Are you tired of the clutter in your home? Are you excited to take steps to change your life for good? Begin your journey now by flipping over to the first chapter.

WHY ARE THERE SO MANY THINGS IN YOUR HOME?

"Don't own so much clutter that you will be relieved to see your house catch fire."

— WENDELL BERRY

A significant problem many individuals face today is that they have too many things in their homes. Books, clothes, shoes, plates, phones, wires, toys, and many more items occupy space in the house and are often never used. These items are what create clutter in the home.

If you understand and accept that this is a fact, then how do you accumulate these items in your home? The answer to this question can be split into three categories. These are the most common reasons why you collect things in your home. Let's quickly explore these reasons.

Purchases Over the Years

Consumerism is a lifestyle that has a significant impact on how consumers behave in the world today. Certain things promote consumerism in the world today. I spent time at a friend's house recently, and there were piles of unsorted clothing from purchases months and years ago. I've seen other homes with two, three, four bottles of the same cleaning solution. So, if you're "collecting" stuff like this, it may be time to examine why.

The first is the possibility of engaging in the mass production of some items, which results in a lower cost of purchase to the consumer. This is an effect of the availability of cheap labor in various countries such as China.

The top-quality marketing strategies in use by various companies today also promotes consumerism. Today, companies choose to target the insecurities of their consumers in a bid to get them to buy products.

Are you a woman, for example, who is conscious of her post-pregnancy stomach? Then companies will choose to advertise waist trainers to help you feel good about your stomach.

These are just some of the strategies in place to encourage consumers to purchase unnecessary products. Combining these strategies with social media, there is very little you can do to avoid coming in contact with these marketing campaigns.

As you give in to these marketing strategies over the years, you steadily pile up possessions that create clutter in the home. Since you believe there will be a time when these items will be useful, you find it difficult to discard them.

Things You Inherited

Another form through which you can acquire a lot of things in your home is through inheritance. In most cases, you also end up with inherited clutter. You can inherit some of these items as a result of any of these:

- If a member of family or friend needs to move to a smaller house or nursing home
- If you lose a loved one, and inherit some of their belongings

In both cases, the items you receive often have a sentimental value that makes it difficult to discard them. A left-over item from an individual that becomes your property is an inheritance. When your grandparents or parents die, it's common for the family to receive their possessions.

A client of mine amassed a large collection of Hummel figurines from her grandmother. They were all over the home, in every nook and cranny she could find. I asked her about them. She said, "Oh, those? I don't even like them. But they were granny's." We talked about how she could safely store them in the garage, and keep out one or two for display as a reminder of her beloved grandmother.

Gifts

Gifts are another means through which you can pile many unnecessary things in your home. Everyone receives a gift now and then, but you may not fancy all the gifts you receive. Despite your dislike for the gift, you may find it difficult to discard the gift. Another friend of mine has a "collection" of sweaters from his mom. He hates all of them, but doesn't have the heart to tell her, or to get rid of them. This is not an uncommon situation.

This is because you don't want to hurt the feelings of the individual giving the gift. Besides, most of us try to avoid getting caught after discarding these gifts. As a result, you end up holding on to something you don't need for long periods.

This action of holding on to gifts might sometimes be due to our lack of understanding of the word gift. For instance, that understanding is also one of the reasons why you might be really uncomfortable saying 'no' to someone giving you a gift. Without saying no, you will continue to accumulate gifts that turn into clutter in your home.

Going by the dictionary definition, a gift is something you receive from another individual without any need for payment. What this implies is that a gift can only remain as one if you have no obligation to the giver. Accounting for their feelings or the fear of discarding is an obligation to the giver that you create.

These obligations make the item you receive stop being a gift. When you understand the meaning of a gift, it becomes easier to let go.

So, why do we collect clutter?

Let's now take a look at some of the reasons we accumulate this type of clutter in our lives. Sit with each of them to see if they resonate with you. Take your time when reading this section – let's get to the root cause of clutter in your life. I'm here to help.

LOW-SELF WORTH

When you take time to break down the strategies various manufacturers utilize in their marketing campaigns, you notice there is a lot of emphasis on making you feel worthless. This is how they get you to buy their products. Through these strategies, and the impact of society today, you adopt the belief that acquiring more possessions can help boost your self-worth.

When you associate more possessions to higher worth, you steadily begin to accumulate clutter in your home. Since you believe your wealth indicates your worth, you use it as a way to overcome your feelings of worthlessness. This is when buying makes you feel better about yourself.

Besides, if you're unable to identify your worth, then you will seek external validation. This will often lead to people-pleasing habits. Due to these habits, you become unable to say no to others.

This is when you start accepting gifts that have no place or use in your home. Souvenirs from friends or gifts from your mother-in-law all find a way into your home to create clutter.

Low self-worth also creates a fear of failure in your life. This fear of failure can also cause an increase in the possessions you have in your home. This is possible when you start worrying about your ability to engage in the act of decluttering successfully.

Despite understanding the benefits of the process, your inability to take the first step towards decluttering will be detrimental.

The Need to Hold on to the Past

There are specific memories you hold dear, and items you associate with these memories. This is common among various individuals. We find it difficult to discard certain things that remind us of our past.

As a parent, watching your kids grow up fast can be overwhelming. Sometimes, you want to remember the times when they were just babies. To recall these memories, you may choose to keep their bed or hold on to drawings from their childhood. These items can serve as triggers for these memories. As triggers, you leave them in your home as keepsakes. Some of these items may be to remind you of times when you were more popular or successful; to help you remember that you should still be proud of yourself.

Other Reasons

In addition to the reasons above, there are other reasons why you may struggle with clutter in your home. For some individuals, the task of decluttering can seem overwhelming. So, they choose to avoid it.

Struggles with a disorder or physical disability can also lead to a pile up of clutter. The hoarding disorder, which I will introduce in the next chapter, is a common issue. In this case, calling a professional can provide a considerable benefit.

Although you may be unwilling to admit it, you might also struggle with clutter due to your lack of proper time-management abilities. This is a skill you must learn, and you don't gain it at birth. Without developing adequate time management abilities, you can never get down to the decluttering process.

Although everyone struggles with one issue or the other, you can always overcome these issues. Now that you know the reasons you're struggling with clutter in your home, it's time to learn about how to deal with them.

The Takeaway

- Clutter is a problem many individuals face which often results from the consumerist lifestyle. Low self-worth often promotes the need to attach worth to the number of possessions you own.
- Memories of the past can prevent you from discarding some old items in the home. Clutter can also result from disorders such as hoarding.
- Many people without time-management skills

and those that struggle with indecision are
prone to have clutter in their houses.

2

CHANGE YOUR PERSPECTIVE ON HOARDING ITEMS

"Hoard food and it rots. Hoard money and you rot. Hoard power and the nation rots."

— CHUCK PALAHNIUK

What is Hoarding?

Hoarding is a compulsion that leads an individual to hold on to things. For an individual with a hoarding disorder, they will find it challenging to throw away or part with any of their possessions. The value of the item in question isn't a factor when it comes to hoarding.

Although many people may consider hoarding to be harmless, it usually has harmful effects. These effects can include:

- Financial: spending excessively on consumer goods, paying for storage, living in a house much bigger than you need.
- Social: difficulty with friends and family members.
- Legal: creating environments where neighbors might complain, or city/municipality codes are being broken.
- Physical: unhealthy living conditions, clutter to an excess where physical space is compromised, unclean, and dangerous.
- Emotional: using physical objects to hold onto emotional difficulties.

THESE EFFECTS of hoarding will affect the hoarder and other individuals he/she interacts with, such as family and friends. You may ask yourself, what is the difference between a hoarder and a regular individual? This is a common question people ask.

To identify a hoarder, the quantity of items in their possession is the most useful factor. These items can occupy entire homes, and make it difficult for other individuals to move around the house. It creates clutter in areas like stairways, desks, countertops, and other surfaces in the home.

The items you can find in possession of a hoarder consist of the following:

- Magazines, newspapers and photographs
- Food items and household items
- Clothing, shoes, and accessories
- Plastic or paper bags and excessive boxes
- Excessive animals, and their "messes."

There are several levels of hoarding into which you can classify hoarders. These levels are known as the "Clutter Hoarding Scale," developed by the National Study Group on Compulsive Disorganization. They include the following:

1. Hoarding Level One: On this level, the clutter is not in excess. The home is still sanitary and safe since there is proper ventilation with no odors, while stairways and doors remain accessible.
2. Hoarding Level Two: Here, you notice garbage cans overflowing with trash while light mildew becomes noticeable in the bathrooms and kitchen. You can find one exit in the home blocked, while there are two or more rooms filled with clutter. There are limited signs of proper housekeeping, light odors, and pet waste or dander puddles present.
3. Hoarding Level Three: The homes on this level have strong odors emanating from them, with noticeable clutter outdoors. Food preparation areas are heavily soiled, and there is an

unusable bathroom or bedroom in the house. You may find too many pets in the home, and there is usually excessive dust.

4. Hoarding Level Four: Counters with rotting food, pet damage around the home, dangerous electrical wiring, sewer backup, flea infestation, and lice on the bedding in the house.

5. Hoarding Level Five: Clutter in the home renders the bathroom and kitchen unusable, utilities such as water and electricity will be disconnected, rodent infestation, and feces of animals and humans around the house.

FROM THESE LEVELS, you can infer that level one is mild, while level five is severe. The level five hoarding will have a significant effect on your daily activities, while the impact of level one hoarding may be insignificant to a great extent.

The issue of hoarding may develop due to compulsion. In this case, compulsive buying, compulsive search, or compulsive acquisition. Compulsive search is noticeable in hoarders who are similar to collectors. These individuals are in search of items that they tag as being unique or perfect, despite these items as being normal to others.

Compulsive buying is identifiable in individuals that always make a purchase anytime they feel it is a bargain. The case of compulsive acquisition refers to individuals that are always looking to get anything that is free. These can be things as useless as flyers.

The presence of the hoarding disorder may be an indicator of another disorder, but in most cases, it is on its own. Other disorders that are indicated by the hoarding disorder include:

- Depression
- Obsessive-Compulsive Disorder (OCD)
- Obsessive-Compulsive Personality disorder (OCPD)
- Attention-deficit/hyperactivity disorder (ADHD)

Hoarding disorder may also be a sign of an eating disorder, although this may be rare. Other disorders associated with hoarding include:

- Prader-Willi syndrome (a genetic disorder resulting in obesity and intellectual disability)
- Dementia
- Pica (intake of non-food materials)
- Psychosis

Who is Likely to Experience it?

An individual with a hoarding disorder can be straightforward to identify. Most of these individuals usually gather a large number of items that create clutter in their homes and find it difficult to discard these items. You can also check for these symptoms:

- Piling up clutter in various rooms until they become unusable
- Gathering items for which there is no storage space or immediate need for
- A compulsion to keep things with a sudden change in mood anytime there is a thought of throwing out these items
- Difficulty engaging in organizing and planning
- Procrastination, avoidance, perfectionism, and indecisiveness
- Social isolation, financial challenges, loss of living space, health hazard, relationship discord
- Embarrassment and feeling overwhelmed by their possessions
- Going through their trash in case they threw out an item by accident
- Always suspicious of other people touching their possessions

Although there are certain similarities between hoarders and collectors, they aren't the same. For collectors, they are intentional in their search for items. They may seek out a specific item such as a model car, or stamps, categorize these items, and put them on display. Another noticeable difference is that collectors organize their things for the purposes of their collection.

Reasons People Hoard

There are different reasons why people hoard items. The following are some reasons to help you understand yourself and other individuals that hoard:

1. You strongly believe that an **item will be of value or use in the future**. These are the items you think you will use later, such as excesses from your last house renovation project or things you think you can sell for a high price in the future, such as collectibles.

2. Your **inability to recall where you stored certain items** in the home can lead to hoarding. When the need for such a thing arises, you buy another on impulse to meet your pressing need. As a result, you have multiple items performing the same function.

3. The idea that an item has **sentimental value** will impulsively make you hoard the item. These items can be photos, books, clothes, and more. Sentimental items are those to which you attach specific memories and emotions.

4. **When you think an item is irreplaceable and unique**, discarding it becomes very difficult. A sweater knitted by your grandmother, something you received

from someone who has passed away, and things that are no longer in production.

5. Depending on the price you got an item, **you may consider it to be a bargain**. This will promote the assumption that you may never be able to get it at such a price in the future. To avoid the possibility of paying more for an item later, you will choose to hold on to it, rather than throw it away.

6. **Indecision** is another reason why you may be hoarding an item. Is it essential or not? When you have a challenge answering this question, you may opt to hold on to the item.

7. You may attach certain events, individuals, and memories in your life to some items in the home. These items assist in jogging your memory about these events or individuals. The belief that **only these items can promote vivid recollection** will lead to hoarding.

Effects of Hoarding

Hoarding is an action that has an impact on you both physically and mentally. The implications of hoarding are noticeable in your environment and your behaviors. In this section, we will focus on various areas in which you can be affected.

Physical Impacts

Hoarding is an action that creates unhealthy living conditions for you. As a hoarder, it will be a challenge to engage in basic daily activities. These include actions like cooking, bathing, and cleaning.

Your inability to perform these actions will affect your hygiene, while your access to a proper diet will be impossible. These lower the effectiveness of your immune system and expose you to illnesses.

When you hoard things, food containers will pile up in the home, and spoiled food will also promote the growth of fungus and mildew. Along with the poor air circulation, you will become a victim of mold problems.

Mold problems can aggravate any existing health problems, trigger your allergies, and also cause damage in your respiratory system.

Pest infestation is another problem you face due to hoarding. With items decomposing in one hidden corner or the other, they become attractive to pests such as rats, ants, flies, cockroaches, and so on.

Since these pests know how to remain hidden, it will be challenging to get them out of the home. This is how the severity of your pest infestation increases over time.

Other Impacts

Hoarding usually affects you mentally. This is identifiable in your struggle with depression, anger, and resentment.

These are often an effect of traumatic or stressful events in your life.

It is also common for hoarders to exhibit social withdrawal. This is because they will usually choose their possessions over their friendships or relationships with others. This can lead to conflict between the hoarder and other individuals.

If you're a hoarder living in a rented apartment with neighbors, you may have been in numerous legal disputes due to your living habits. Neighbors complain about the pests, dirt, and smell that generate from your home. Don't assume the world is against you, but see this as a push for you to make a change.

Hoarders also go through financial difficulties that never seem to go away. This is an outcome of their inability to separate valuable items from those that are worthless. Your purchases as a hoarder are to get something new to grow your collection. Also, you may find yourself having challenges keeping a job or even getting one.

Your safety is also at risk as a hoarder. This is because you may be living in buildings with structural damage or using appliances that are damaged. Since you find it difficult to let a professional come into your home and take a look, you choose to leave things as they are.

It would help if you understood that faulty electronics, stoves, and other appliances have a high risk of resulting in a fire. Once a fire starts, it will quickly spread to other areas of the home since your collection will consist of highly flammable objects.

The Takeaway

- Hoarding is a disorder in which an individual is compelled to hold on to things.
- Hoarding can affect you financially, emotionally, legally, socially, and physically.
- Compulsive buying, compulsive search, and compulsive acquisitions are different compulsions that result in hoarding
- The symptoms of hoarding may indicate depression, obsessive-compulsive disorder (OCD), obsessive-compulsive personality disorder (OCPD), and attention-deficit-hyperactivity disorder (ADHD). It can also indicate psychosis, dementia, pica, and Prader Willi syndrome.
- Hoarding is noticeable in individuals of all ages and becomes more severe the older an individual gets.
- Hoarders may be exposed to dangers such as structural damage, pest infestation, stress, depression, and more.

3

MINIMALISM AND DANSHARI

"The first step in crafting the life you want is to get rid of everything you don't."

— JOSHUA BECKER

What is Danshari?

Decluttering is an art, some would argue. It's not as simple as throwing things away, or not collecting things in the first place. The mantra, "less is more," applies when decluttering, and Danshari is a way to wrap your mind and heart about the decluttering process.

Many of us are more familiar with this concept through two prominent Japanese minimalists; Fume Sasaki, who lives in a tiny house with only 150 "possessions," and Marie Kondo, the recent Netflix star and purveyor of keeping things that "spark joy." But, Danshari is much more than these two individuals.

In many ways, Danshari is inspired by the Shinto religion, which focuses on the energy of all things around us. Shinto, in this context, is about "treasuring what you have; treating the objects you own a disposable, but valuable, no matter their actual monetary worth; and creating displays so you can value each individual object are all essentially Shinto ways of living." (Dilloway, 2019)

In its simplest form, Danshari consists of three Japanese Kanji (or symbols) which mean:

- Refuse (Dan)
- Throw away (Sha)
- Separate (Ri)

Dan – To Refuse

To refuse means you should limit the flow of items into your home and life. You have to be excellent at this job to reduce the clutter in your life. There are various actions to take if you want to refuse. Now, this might seem difficult, and at first it is. But, when we give our friends and family members other options, it can make everyone feel at ease.

For example, you can start by distributing a gift exemption certificate. By sending this certificate, you can let your friends and family know that rather than exchanging gifts, you will prefer other ways for both parties to relish the season.

You can also take other actions, such as:

- Asking for good deeds such as car washing, snow shoveling, etc. in place of gifts
- Propose a donation to your favorite charity, or a charity of their choice
- Bring up the idea of a gift-free holiday like doing kind things for each other
- Letting them know that time spent together is the best gift of all

These are just a few, and there are many other actions you can take to avoid gifts.

Another step to take in refusal is to avoid collecting freebies. Samples and trials are popular things that just create clutter in your home. These can be in the form of calendars, pens, notebooks, or magnets, all with a company name. Being polite is one of the reasons why you often collect these freebies, but you can also learn to decline politely.

Choosing minimalism is another way to achieve refusal. It helps you reduce your consumption to only your needs.

Sha – To Throw Away

This is another step that helps simplify your life. This is a crucial part of the decluttering process in which you discard unnecessary items in your home. There are some simple actions you can take to apply this in your life effectively.

You can start by adopting the idea of discarding one

item a day. This is a much simpler and faster way to engage in decluttering. The item you choose to discard can be anything in the home. As long as you're not bringing any new item in, you will see noticeable changes in the house.

Some items that you feel can still be useful should go into a donation box that you can store in your garage. This is to make it easier to move when it is time to donate.

It can really clear your mind, heart and spirit to "let go" of things that you're holding onto – with love. For example, you can give heirlooms to other members of your extended family or donate them to a charitable organization. You can also take a photo of something that is very special to you before you let it go; sometimes that makes it easier. I also recommend selling them yourself, and then donating the money or using it for something essential to you.

If you're holding on to an item of historical value, then you can boost the inventory of a university or museum around you. For collections, you can save just a piece or two for yourself. A friend of mine recently moved overseas, and had to leave most of her book collection in the United States. She chose ten of her favorite books to bring with her. You can go through a similar exercise with any collectibles - save your absolute favorites, and limit them to a low number, donating or selling the rest.

The best option is usually to avoid collecting these heirlooms in the first place. As you do this, also remember the things in your wardrobe and kitchen.

- Clothes that don't fit

- Appliances and pans you don't use
- Clothes you don't wear
- Shoes and purses you don't wear or use more than a few times a year

ALL THESE AND other items you find should leave the home. Go through your storage rooms and other places in your home and bring out all the things you don't need. Donate things to local charities, or places where they can use items. For example, in my town, there are domestic violence and homeless shelters that are always appreciative of items that can go to help those in need.

Ri – To Separate

This is the last part, and it involves eliminating any form of attachment you have with any possessions in your home. Learning to do this is simple, and there are some tips to help.

The first tip is to learn to appreciate your space. You should understand that not only does possession create clutter, but clutter also occupies your space. Understanding that space creates room for creativity can be of help.

With clutter around, you're only going to struggle with discord and chaos. To engage in the process of separation, you need to start anew. In the process of decluttering, this involves bringing out everything you own and then letting in only those that you're sure you cherish and need.

For instance, you can choose to discard your current schedule and create a new one. On this new schedule, you make sure you slot in only activities that add to your life in one way or the other.

In the case of your possessions, keep only the essential items, and be sure they are in their appropriate storage locations. Nothing should be on your countertops, and make use of drawers and cabinets.

You must understand that the concept of Danshari also encompasses your mental clutter in addition to physical clutter.

Less is More – Danshari Mantra

The concept of "less is more" is the focal of how we can think and feel when decluttering our lives, using the methods discussed in this book. In life, we tend to get caught up in excesses, for many reasons. The discipline that can be developed by thinking, seeing and feeling that "less is more," can be quite freeing. This concept is noticeable in both Danshari and Wabi-Sabi.

Many advocates of the Danshari minimalist lifestyle included Steve Jobs, Marie Kondo (who we've mentioned), and Buddhist or Zen monks.

Another important concept that relates to Danshari is "Wabi-Sabi." This is a Japanese concept that also promotes the idea that less is more. "Wabi" can mean an "understated elegance," while "Sabi" means "accepting imperfections with pleasure."

This concept accepts three things in life. These are:

- Nothing is perfect
- Nothing is finished
- Nothing lasts

THROUGH AN UNDERSTANDING OF WABI-SABI, you can appreciate things the way they are, rather than focusing on how they should be. The acceptance of imperfection is in contrast to the constant pursuit of perfection, which is prevalent all around us.

This is the pursuit of relationships, achievements, and possessions. In the end, all you end up with is depression, stress, hasty judgment, and anxiety.

Why Should You Accept it?

As we've discussed, the notion of decluttering is not just about "stuff" in your home, car or workspace. The "stuff" we collect often goes much deeper than that. So, the notion of "less is more," can help clear our hearts, minds and spirits...as well as our home of needless clutter.

Let's take a look at a few reasons to explore how this mindset can benefit you.

IT GRANTS EMOTIONAL Relief

In life, various things lead to emotional turmoil. One of the most common is when you lose your possessions. This can be due to a fire outbreak or a natural disaster.

The concept of less is more promotes the idea of having less emotional attachment to your possessions and other aspects of life. As a result, you're less likely to experience an emotional breakdown in the event of any loss of property. Although it may be going too far, some individuals also apply this concept to their relationship with others.

This is a means through which you can avoid being under the control of past events or emotions.

IT PROMOTES BACKPACKING

As we discussed in the previous chapter, a severe issue that leads to clutter is hoarding. The opposite of hoarding is backpacking. This is one thing you adopt when you learn that less is more.

The lifestyle of a backpacker involves traveling around the world without anything but a backpack. The items in this backpack are all the possessions you own. As a backpacker, you value memories and experiences over the accumulation of possessions.

The fewer possessions you own, the better your mobility.

IT PROMOTES DECLUTTERING

This should be a no-brainer. When you accept to live with less, you begin to discard your excesses. You may not recognize that you're a hoarder, but if you have things around the home that you never use, then you're one.

. . .

You Control Your Words

The idea of less is more also extends to your words. When you talk too much, you run the risk of getting into trouble. You may even end up exposing things you shouldn't.

In your relationship with others, learning that less is more can prevent you from causing conflict. You learn to say only the things you need to. A few words can help you get your point across without things escalating into a full-blown argument.

The Takeaway

- Danshari is a Japanese word that translates to decluttering. It is made up of three Japanese kanji. You can split the word Danshari into Dan, Sha, and Ri.
- Dan means to refuse. It implies that you need to limit the flow of items into your home and life.
- Sha means to throw away. This means that you must be willing to discard all the unnecessary items in your possession.
- Ri means to separate. This means that you break off the attachment you have with your possessions as this hinders your ability to discard

- The Danshari mantra is "less is more."
- There are several reasons why you should accept this mantra including the emotional relief it grants. The mantra also promotes decluttering and the backpacking lifestyle.

4

HOW TO APPLY DANSHARI TO YOUR LIFE

"Instead of thinking I am losing something when I clear clutter, I dwell on what I might gain."

— LISA J. SHULTZ

There are times when you experience challenges and pressure in life. These situations can create both mental and physical clutter, depending on the extent to which they affect you. For many individuals, Danshari practice can provide an escape from these situations.

Most of the challenges and stress you go through are often a result of your lifestyle. When living a consumerist lifestyle, you're burdened with the need to acquire possessions. For many individuals, they end up deep in debt due to the need to live the consumerist lifestyle.

As you acquire more possessions, they occupy most of

the living area in your home. The lack of space in your home hinders your creativity and productivity while creating stress in your life.

These are some of the issues you can solve through the danshari practice. Despite its effectiveness, you must submit yourself entirely to the practice. You will end up wasting your time and energy if you begin the process half-heartedly.

This can make you feel more frustrated, stressed, and confused than you were before. If you're ready to take action, let's move on to the next section.

How To Start Your Danshari Practice

The Danshari practice is crucial to your success in maintaining a clutter-free lifestyle. To start this practice, I will give you some steps you can take. Read on!

COMMIT to Your New Minimalist Lifestyle

The minimalist lifestyle is necessary for the Danshari practice. Since Danshari involves getting rid of clutter, you must be willing to live your life with whatever is left over after the decluttering process.

To commit to this new lifestyle, you must first understand your worth as an individual. When you learn your worth, you will break free of the common notion that your possessions indicate your worth. Assessing your real value and self-worth will make it possible to let go of the attachment you have to your belongings.

The minimalist lifestyle also involves learning to stop overcommitting. Go through your priorities again. Find out the areas creating issues in your life.

- Do you visit too many people?
- Are you always accepting requests from others?
- Are you committing to things that stray away from your priorities?

By assessing your life and actions, you can find out the areas where you spend most of your time and energy.

An inward look at yourself can also promote a shift towards the minimalist mindset. You can ask yourself these questions:

- Can I attain satisfaction without owning too many possessions?
- Am I happy with who I am?

To know we're happy with who we are, we must take away all the material possessions before assessing ourselves. This will give us the option to evaluate our true selves. This is not an easy path, but one that benefits us in a million different ways.

We must also assess the possibility of attaining satisfaction without having excess possessions. This is the moment when we learn to place value on experiences and relationships over possessions.

Looking inwardly, you get to know that all you are is a collection of your experiences and the memories you make.

Through this understanding, you can understand that possessions add nothing to these experiences and memories. It is the people you spend your time with and how you spend your time.

Don't Focus on What You're Losing

If you choose to focus on what you're losing, you will never be able to let go of your possessions. To change your focus, you must change the way you think about Danshari. This is a concept that promotes the idea of being happy with who you are as an individual.

You must also understand that Danshari isn't just about living with fewer things. It helps you overcome the mindset in which you believe that your happiness depends on what you own.

A friend of mine recently moved from the central United States to Mexico. She was limited to one van of possessions she could bring with her, and that included her two dogs and a cat. She chose to bring only one suitcase of clothing, original artwork, one-of-a-kind furniture that she dismantled to fit, and utilitarian folding furniture that she could use when she arrived at her empty, non-furnished place in Mexico.

Instead of lamenting on what she had left behind, "I felt a freedom that I hadn't felt in decades. Paring down my belonging only to the bare essentials, what would fit in that van, was incredibly refreshing. And, I was doing it to start a new, exciting life."

Eliminate the Things You Don't Need

To fully adopt the Danshari practice, you need to start getting rid of the things you don't need. You can start from one item at a time, and then move on to full-scale decluttering.

Letting go of your possessions is difficult, so you have to slide into it gently. Sometimes this process brings up tears, or laughter, or both. It's ok to feel those emotions as you go. If it becomes difficult, you can start with the most obvious clutter in your house. This can be old clothes or broken appliances. Things that don't bring up as many emotions.

What is most important is that you start now. This will give you enough time to develop and accept this new habit.

When you make a bold decision to go on with the full-scale decluttering process, you still need to be thoughtful in your actions. You must separate the necessary items from those that you no longer need.

For example, with your seasonal items, you should do away with things you time. Looking at items like Christmas decorations in September will have you thinking of the last time you used them, but by December, you're going to need them.

Decluttering can be an emotional process, depending on your approach. For individuals that choose to throw these items in the trash, it can be a considerable challenge. This is why you should always try other options first.

You can decide to hold a yard sale, donate to charity, or sell them online. If the thought of decluttering is an issue due to the money you spent on these items, then the opportunity to sell these items will make it less painful.

The Takeaway

- Danshari is a way to escape the stress and challenges you face in life.
- It minimizes stress through the clutter you eliminate, and you can overcome financial difficulties if you choose to sell and stop buying on impulse.
- To apply Danshari in your life, you must commit to minimalism.
- Committing to minimalism involves assessing the various actions you take in life.
- You must be willing to shift your focus from the things you lose to what you gain if you want to apply Danshari in your life successfully.
- Learning to let go of what you don't need is crucial in Danshari.

5

UNSTUFF YOUR ROOMS

"You don't have to face every skeleton in your closet before you can make some room in there!"

— CARMEN KLASSEN

Decluttering Is a State of Mind

Your new lifestyle of minimalism is dependent on your willingness to accept and engage in the decluttering process. It is a new state of mind that you must adopt. A state of mind in which you appreciate the space that you create by eliminating clutter.

To be successful in the process of decluttering, you must go beyond saying, "I will declutter." Instead, you should start believing in the process of decluttering. This implies that you believe that the decluttering process will work for you, and help you develop a better life.

There are ways to help you develop this belief in the decluttering process. One of these is to think about the improvements you will experience in your quality of life. Creating a list of what you intend to achieve through the decluttering process is also very helpful. When you create this list, it is similar to writing out your goals. Having goals will motivate you to push forward when things get complicated.

Take out a piece of paper, and draw three columns with the following labels:

1. Decluttering will help me practically, by...
2. Decluttering will help me spiritually/emotionally, by...
3. Decluttering might be difficult for me, because...

Really sit with the exercise while you fill out those columns. Take your time, and understand where your emotions might be coming from. To have benefit beyond your immediate decluttering efforts, it's critical that you examine things a little deeper than you might have in the past. We all benefit when we look at ourselves this way, even if it's uncomfortable.

As I've talked about throughout this book, and the other related books that I've written on this topic, the decluttering process is a long-term experience. Many people find it easy to "give up" when they have to act for an extended period. But, try to avoid that trap. Keeping your goals in focus will enable you to stick with the long-term decluttering process.

Also, having a plan is necessary. Without a plan, you will keep running in circles without making any progress. Your plan is a guide to get you to your destination. The simple notes you take to identify how decluttering will help you, in all aspects of your life, can help keep you motivated and focused on the deeper reasons why decluttering can be so beneficial to you.

There is a sequential approach to completing the decluttering process and achieving the goals you set. Let's take a look at how you can declutter, room by room, area by area.

How To Unstuff Your Home

To unstuff your home, there are some actions you can take. You can think of these as the initial steps to ease the process of decluttering. These actions are applicable to all areas of the home.

START by Eliminating Things You Don't Need or Want

You can fast-track the decluttering process by your actions during the initial stages. When going through your possessions, it is easy to identify the things you no longer need and those you don't want.

These are the items you should declutter first. Some things that fit this category include:

- Old clothes that do not fit, or that are worn-out
- Old magazines
- Old or broken appliances
- Old furniture
- Shoes that no longer fit
- Children's toys
- Sentimental items
- Gifts you don't want

There are many more items that fit into this category, and you will quickly identify them when going through your possessions. Toss them out as soon as you identify them.

You can have a box for those that will go into the trash can and another for those you will donate. This is an organizational trick that will save you any additional stress in the future.

Once you're able to separate these items, you're left with those you feel you need. You should understand that these items will still contain clutter. When organizing what's left, be sure to choose only the things that are essential to you.

This is an action that will help you cut down on the clutter in your home.

CLEAR ALL SURFACES

In every home, it is common to find different items taking up space on different surfaces. These surfaces include those in your living room, dining room, office, bedroom, kitchen, and so on. Although these may be essential items, you should consider them as clutter if they are not in their proper storage area.

The surfaces you should check during this process include the desk in your home office, kitchen countertops, sinks, dining table, ottoman, center table, and so on. Items that appear to be unnecessary should be moved off these surfaces.

Shred Old Letters and Recycle Junk Mail

Your old letters create paper clutter in your home. These can occupy space on a surface in the house or a drawer. Letters from a friend, a job applicant, those from service companies, your bank, and so on, all create paper clutter in the home.

Since paper is very light, you can have them flying around and littering the home as a result of wind. You can eliminate this form of clutter by shredding them. Shredding is a safer way of getting rid of paper clutter since it may contain some of your vital details. You don't want anyone going through your trash and finding out personal information.

If shredding isn't the right option, then you can choose to recycle junk mail. Various paper products, such as glossy paper can be recycled. Although you can recycle as it is, you can make an effort to remove the plastic windows on any envelope you want to recycle.

Be sure to keep the paper dry and remove your address labels before recycling. Things like paper labels and plastics (if it comes with your credit card) can contaminate paper recycling, so be sure to eliminate them.

Shredded paper often can't be recycled, so you must find a way to dispose of them properly.

Important papers can be filed away neatly. If the originals aren't needed, but you still want to keep the "paper," you can take a photo or scan the important document and keep a virtual file.

Discard Old Ornaments or Decorations

There are ornaments you may be hoarding in your home but never use. These will include those you bought during a family holiday one or two decades ago. Why do you still have them?

Many individuals will argue that these items serve as triggers for some of their important memories. This isn't a compelling argument. Take this time to try taking a photo of the item in question, does the picture trigger the same memory?

A few years ago, I went through a large box of photos and items that were sentimental to me. I wanted to get rid of the box, so I took the time to take pictures of things that meant something to me, and threw out the box. But within a week, my laptop was stolen. Everything that I had photographed was on that computer, and I had no backup. I was crushed, and lamented my loss.

Two months later, do you think I can remember what was lost? Do I remember the specific photos and items? No. But the memories are there, and I know that the experiences, even if never remembered, have shaped who I am today – so the memento doesn't mean as much as how things shaped my life.

I know it will, so there is no need to have the physical item around, and occupying your space. Your memories are stored in your brain, so without the item or not, you will still have these memories.

THROW Out Expired Products

Your freezer or fridge does an excellent job in helping you preserve your foodstuffs. Sometimes, maybe they do too much. Since you're sure of the effectiveness of these appliances, it is easy to keep items past their expiration.

At this moment, you must go through all the products in your freezer and fridge. Look for those that have been there for too long, and those that have expired. It would be best if you threw them out quickly to avoid consuming anything that can damage your health.

This check must go beyond your fridge or freezer. Check your kitchen cabinets and other food storage areas. Canned food, spices, and other items beyond their expiry date should be discarded.

You can also separate those that are close to expiry. If you're sure you won't be able to use these items before the expiry date, then look for a way to give them out. You can ask friends and family or search for where they will be put to use. Wasting food isn't a great thing, so make sure to donate as much as you can and reduce your purchases to the essentials.

Use Vacuum Storage Bags

To save storage space, vacuum storage bags are excellent. Nonetheless, you must be cautious when using this form of storage. First, you must avoid sealing clothes for too long.

This is to avoid damage to the fabric due to the absence of air in the storage bag. For items that are special and delicate, such as a wedding dress, you should look for other storage options such as plastic containers.

To use the vacuum storage bags, you can choose to roll-up clothes instead of folding. This will help prevent the clothes from creasing while in storage.

Since the bags are fragile, look for a place to store them away from sharp objects. This will prevent them from getting punctured and allow you to reuse them.

You can choose this storage option for some of your accessories, and out of season clothes. When these items are needed, you can break them out of storage.

The Takeaway

- Decluttering is a state of mind.

- There are several steps you can take to declutter the rooms in your home.
- Be sure to clear all surfaces and discard old magazines or documents.
- Old ornaments and expired products shouldn't have a place in your house.
- Use vacuum storage bags to save space in your closet.

6

PUBLIC LIVING SPACES

"Clear your stuff. Clear your mind."

— ERIC M. RIDDLE

Public spaces in the home are those areas where anyone can access without any restrictions. They include your living room, dining room, and kitchen. These are the areas we will be looking at in this chapter.

Kitchen

One of the few public spaces in your home that is a hub for clutter is your kitchen. Foodstuffs, plates, cups, and appliances are some of the things responsible for clutter in the kitchen. You can get rid of clutter through these actions:

. . .

CLEAR OUT CUPBOARDS

Since cupboards are essential to storing items, it's good to spend some time clearing out excess. Since items in cupboards are "out of sight, out of mind," it's common to pile them up with unnecessary things. In clearing your cupboard, make sure you're getting rid of duplicate or unused items.

Reduce the number of plates, pots, and cups in the cupboards. For easy organization, limit the number of plates and cups to just enough to get you through a day or two. For a family, include a set for each family member.

I recommend making it enough for a day, so you have no option but to do your dishes on a daily basis. Removing duplicates will increase the storage space available for use. When arranging pots, put them all in one cupboard.

You should invert the lids so there is the option of stacking. Also, similar items should be stored together. All plates should be in the same cupboard, cups should be in a separate cupboard, and you can have your cutlery sets in a drawer.

REARRANGE APPLIANCES

There are certain appliances that need to be in the kitchen. Some have to be on surfaces, while others should be in storage. Separate your appliances into categories, and organize them.

Your coffee maker and microwave are appliances that should have a place on the kitchen surface, for example, if you use them every day. Your food processor, blender, and electric grill are other useful appliances that can be in a storage compartment. You can easily get them out when you need them.

You may have appliances you don't use in the kitchen sitting on countertops. This is when you need to move these appliances to their appropriate storage locations.

INGREDIENTS AND CEREALS

Go through your jars of herbs and spices first to find those that are expired, as we discussed previously. You don't want to make the mistake of feeding your family these ingredients. Throw them out to create more space.

Mason jars are excellent for the purpose of storing herbs, spices, and cereals. The transparency of these jars also makes it easy to know when you're running low.

For ingredients and other utensils you use only on special occasions, you can dedicate a drawer or cupboard for the storage of these types of items. This might be a drawer or nook you will open less often, so you must check the expiration date before using any item here.

Remember, your kitchen surfaces and countertops should be free of clutter. Anytime you return from grocery shopping, put each item in its proper storage location and not on countertops.

Living Room

Your living room is a place for your everyday use. It is the gathering room for every member of your family. You can choose to watch television, read a book, go through magazines, or just have a chat in the living room.

The versatility of the living room provides an opportunity for clutter to pile up. Here are some of the things that create clutter in the living room and how to deal with them.

Books

When relaxing in the living room, you can choose to read a book or magazine. Since you may not complete the book on the same day, you may decide to place it on the table in the living room. This is in preparation for the next time you read.

Following your action, other family members may end up placing books on the same table. Soon, you will have a cluttered table. You can also have stacks of magazines on the floor in the living room.

To curb this form of clutter, you can install a bookshelf in the living room. This can be a standing bookcase or wall bookcase.

Being Smart with Furniture

One option to minimize clutter in the living room is to increase your storage options. You can make the most of your furniture by searching for those that serve multiple purposes. An example is an ottoman.

Depending on the ottoman you purchase, you can get a surface to sit or place items along with internal storage space. This internal storage will be useful in storing remotes, magazines, and TV guides.

Buy Baskets and Bags

Baskets and bags are useful storage solutions you can have in the living room. Do you have blankets, pillows and other throws lying about in your living room or elsewhere in our house? How do you store these items? After you declutter items you don't need or use, you can use baskets to store things like blankets, seasonal clothing, towels, etc.

Discarding CDs and DVDs

DVDs and CDs are items that create a challenge when you need to decide to keep or discard. You may choose to keep certain DVDs or CDs, but never play them again. In the meantime, they're creating clutter. They don't have any monetary value, generally. Plus, so much is now available online through streaming services, there's no need to have a physical copy.

This will create clutter in the home that can pile up over the years. Take time today to go through these items. Identify those you will never open or watch again, and discard or donate them.

Rearrange

Rearranging the furniture in your living room is one

way to create space. This can also be a means through which you discover all the toys left behind by your kids. You can use a basket to store these toys when you find them.

The arrangement you choose for your living room is important. Go online and search various minimalist designs you can use in your home.

DINING ROOM

The size of your dining table determines the amount of space you have left in your dining room. One question you should ask yourself is if you actually need that size of the table.

- Are you eight in your family?
- Do you entertain guests often?

Answering these two questions is an excellent way to determine the dining table size you need. If you can get by with four seats, then change to a dining table for four. This creates more space and you have nothing to lose.

Develop New Habits

The next thing to do is to develop healthy cleaning habits. These are habits to help prevent pile up of clutter in your dining room, including clearing placemats and coasters off the table after each meal.

This improves the appearance of your dining room and

leaves it clutter-free. If your dining room contains drawers and cupboards, then use them effectively. Cans and bottles should be put away, and learn to leave your countertops clear.

Dining rooms provide a good space for families to bond. In my family, we use our dining room to engage in fun activities like playing board games, assembling jigsaw puzzles and more. We've spent hours putting together our annual Christmas holiday puzzle, and playing the game of "Life!" If you do the same, then you should understand the level of clutter these create.

Always remember to put them into storage as soon as you finish the activity for the day. You may need to think of an alternative when you're short on storage space. You can search for portable or travel versions of these board games to minimize the space they occupy. They are still fun to play, but smaller.

The Takeaway

- Public living spaces are accessible by any member of the family. These areas include your kitchen, living room, and dining room.
- To clear clutter in your kitchen, you need to clear out your cupboards. Rearrange the appliances in the kitchen, and move out those appliances that shouldn't be there.
- The living room accumulates clutter in the form of books, magazines, CDs, DVDs, and so

on. Install a bookshelf to store books and magazines in your living room.

- Get baskets and bags for storage.
- To clear the clutter in your dining room, you can purchase a smaller dining table to save space.
- Develop new habits of keeping the house clean and decluttered.

7

PRIVATE LIVING SPACES

"You're the boss of clutter, not the other way around."

— MONIKA KRISTOFFERSON

P rivate spaces are places that are accessible only to select members of the family. These are places where you go when you need to recharge and rest.

Bedroom

The bedroom is a place of rest at the end of the day. Creating clutter in your bedroom will have a negative effect on your health. The clutter in your bedroom encourages feelings of guilt.

You might even feel guilty because you assume you're

avoiding the job of eliminating clutter. This guilt creates tension which can induce stress in your life. One of the effects of stress is trouble falling asleep. When we have clutter in our homes, it's a symptom of clutter in our minds. This can keep us awake at night; tossing and turning as thoughts and concerns keep us awake. This emotional clutter shows up in many ways, and insomnia is not uncommon when we're dealing with "clutter."

To avoid these issues, you must take steps to declutter your bedroom, and also avoid the pile up of clutter in the future. You can take these steps to minimize clutter in your bedroom.

Develop New Habits

The first action you must take in controlling clutter in your bedroom is to develop new habits. These habits include putting clothes away each night, and storing shoes properly.

Shoes and clothes are common items that create clutter in the bedroom. When you get home tired, you just want to take off your clothes and rest. At this moment, you're not interested in where your clothes land or where you pull off your shoes.

You can make it a habit to arrange these clothes and shoes before jumping on your bed. If you're going to take a short nap, then you can arrange these items properly when you wake up later in the day. The goal is to ensure there are no clothes or shoes scattered across the room before you go to bed.

. . .

Go **Through Drawers and Wardrobes**

These are storage spaces where you may find the most clutter in your bedroom. You must be ruthless if you want to discard unnecessary items in your wardrobe and drawers.

Clothes that you don't wear any longer, and those that don't fit should be discarded. If the clothes are in excellent condition, then you can donate them to people that will appreciate it more.

Store Out-of-Season Clothes **Properly**

These are clothes that may occupy crucial space in your wardrobe. Since they won't be used for a while, then you can have a special storage for these clothes. You can get a plastic storage container and fold these clothes in.

Once you have them in containers, then you can move these containers under your bed, or place them on the top of your wardrobe. When it's autumn, move your summer/spring outfits into storage.

Repeat the process based on the current season, and you will notice an improvement in your wardrobe.

Organize **the Bags**

Bags in your bedroom include paper bags, plastic bags, reusable shopping bags, and traveling bags. You can move the traveling bag to a storage room until the next time you need it.

For the shopping bags, plastic bags, and paper bags, you can find a larger bag to store them. Fold them neatly so they occupy less space and are well organized.

Get a Hamper for Dirty Clothes

The hamper will serve as a laundry basket in your room. Since dirty clothes create the most clutter in your bedroom, then having somewhere to put them saves you a lot of trouble.

It doesn't have to be a hamper. You can get any other basket for this purpose. Finding one that matches the decoration of your bedroom is the best action to take.

Declutter the Distractions

Distractions in your bedroom usually come from the various devices in your bedroom. Consider getting ridding rid of, and banning anything with a screen from your bedroom. Smartphones, TV, and computers are some of the devices you might want to exclude. Take your bedroom from "digital" to "analog" to reduce these distracting devices.

Get yourself a classic alarm clock and read a book when on your bed. Limit your computer use to your home office, and charge your smartphone outside. While television may seem like a good idea for your bedroom, it is part of the reason you may struggle to fall asleep at night.

· · ·

GET RID of Containers

When you use makeup and moisturizers, you may end up having multiple half-used bottles on your dresser. These containers create clutter in your bedroom. Throwing them out is your next step.

To get to the point when you can throw them out, you have to use the contents of these containers. If there is any container you're sure you won't use, then find someone to give it to, or discard it.

STORE ACCESSORIES in Bowls and Trays

Having a place to store your accessories is necessary to reduce clutter. You can create a storage space using a bowl or a tray. When you take off these accessories, simply place them into the bowl or on the tray.

Glasses, loose change, and keys are some things you can store in a tray. Jewelry like earrings and watches fit better in a bowl.

Bathroom

Your bathroom can get messy quickly if you don't make an effort to control clutter. Although it may be the smallest room in your home, it is used by everyone in the home. There are different items you pile up in the bathroom, and you need to start getting rid of them now.

The following actions will help you declutter your bathroom in a short time:

. . .

Leave Only Daily Use Products

To minimize clutter in your bathroom, make sure only the products you need daily are stored. These products include toothpaste, toothbrush, shampoo, soap, and so on.

Install a Hanging Shelf

Hanging shelves offer an excellent solution to your storage problem. This is because you can install them in places that would otherwise be impossible to use. For example, you can try installing a hanging shelf above your bathroom door.

You can use this shelf when you need to store extra products. These include shampoos, toilet paper, soaps, and other supplies.

Control Cord Clutter

There are certain appliances you need in your bathroom. Your curling iron and hair dryer are just a few of these appliances. The cords on these appliances can create clutter in your bathroom.

To control this clutter, you can start by searching for cordless appliances. If these are unavailable, then get a basket to store these appliances. All you need is a small-sized basket where you can place these appliances, before storing them out of sight.

I recommend using a magazine rack or file organizer for this purpose. You can attach these to the inside of a cabinet door or the side of the sink. This will help save the space under your sink.

Throw Out Expired Products

If you have a medicine cabinet in your bathroom, then this is the right time to go through the items in this cabinet. Check the expiration date on each product, and discard it when necessary.

In addition to medicine, you should also go through your makeup drawers. Throw out anything that is past expiration. When trying to organize these items back into their storage spaces, you can make use of dividers to separate the drawers. This will reduce the stress you go through when searching for items.

Separate and Combine Cleaning Products and Personal Hygiene Products

This is an organizational tip that is also geared towards your safety, since you want to make sure you keep any toxic cleaning products away from children or pets. But, beyond that, by organizing these items separately, you'll find that overall clutter is reduced. Especially when you combine duplicate bottles of glass cleaner, like I found at a client's home. Between the bottles under the bathroom sinks, kitchen sinks, and in the pantry – 7 bottles were combined to just one.

Same with personal hygiene products. Two partially used bottles of body lotion were combined to one, three same-brand shampoo bottles into one, and four bottles of same-brand liquid soap were integrated into two.

The Takeaway

- Your private spaces can serve as getaway areas when you need to be alone, rest, and recharge. The bedroom and bathroom are the two main private areas.
- Your bedroom is one place where you create a lot of clutter, and the clutter here also has a significant impact on you.
- Remove all distractions like TVs, laptops, and phones from the bedroom.
- When decluttering your bathroom, make sure you clear out expired products.
- Utilize bathroom space efficiently by introducing hanging shelves.
- Separate your cleaning products from personal hygiene products for safety

8

STORAGE SPACES

"If someone doesn't live with you, neither should their stuff."

— MONIKA KRISTOFFERSON

Storage spaces in your home include your garage, shed, and loft spaces or attic. For most individuals, these areas serve as the best places to dump things that may be useful in the future. Some of these items do turn out useful, but most don't.

Regardless of what may happen in the future, you can take steps to organize and declutter your storage spaces today. There are different actions you can take to achieve the results you desire.

The actions I discuss in this chapter are applicable to all storage spaces in the home.

. . .

Clear Out the Space

To perform a thorough job when decluttering and organizing storage spaces, your first step must be to take everything out. Depending on the items in storage, this may be a challenge.

If you have items that will be too difficult to move on your own, then get someone to assist you. Don't try moving heavy objects alone. You may end up hurting yourself in the process.

Discard Duplicates

There are certain items you use on rare occasions. Due to the frequency of their use, you may forget where you store them. The next time you need them, you often have to get another piece.

When you come across duplicates of an item, then you must discard the excesses. You can donate these items, or sell it to someone who needs it.

Store Similar Items Together

Storage spaces like your garage and sheds are often used in storing gardening tools, sporting equipment, technical tools, hardware, and so on. When organizing these storage spaces, put these items together.

If you're storing them in containers, arrange the

containers together. This will ease the process of finding your tools when you need them.

Use Labels

Labeling boxes and storage containers is a time-saving trick to apply during the decluttering process. With labels, you can easily find what you need anytime you head to your storage space.

Install Shelves

To efficiently use the space in your garage or shed, then you need to introduce shelves. Shelving is a way to utilize the surfaces above the ground.

There are shelves useful for storing sporting equipment, gear, and accessories. There are different designs depending on what you intend to store. You can find shelves for your soccer balls, in-line skates, basketballs, skis, and so on.

If you enjoy DIY projects, then don't shy away from creating storage shelves on your own.

Install Hooks, Racks and Clips

In addition to shelves, you can also use hooks and clips to store some items off the ground. Bicycles and gardening tools are some things you can store on these hooks and clips.

Bicycles can also be stored on sturdy racks if you prefer these to clips. You can get these at accessory stores around you. There should be wall studs into which you can fasten the racks.

Separate Your Space into Zones

Creating zones in your garage, shed, or loft will make things a lot easier. In your garage, you can have a separate zone for power tools, another for sporting equipment and protective gear, and another for gardening tools.

It is vital you store the protective gear near sporting equipment since they are usually used together. You can assign this zone close to where you park your car, along with the zone for camping gear.

This is to ease the process of loading and unloading these items into your vehicle.

Use Jars for Sharp Objects

Since you may find yourself performing some DIY projects in your garage or shed, there will be loose screws and nails lying around. These are hazards that can cause injury to anyone living in the house.

You can use jars to keep these objects secure. These jars can be arranged on the shelves in the storage space, and can come in handy during your next project.

. . .

Choose Storage Containers **Wisely**

The storage containers you use in your storage units can create clutter. If you have a mix of boxes, plastic containers, and other storage options, then you will have difficulties arranging or stacking them. You can choose to either use plastic containers or boxes when storing your possessions.

I recommend the use of plastic storage containers since they last longer and can easily be stacked. This will help save space in your home.

Dismantle **Your Furniture**

Before moving furniture into storage spaces, it is a good idea to dismantle the furniture. If you're moving an old desk, bed, dining set, or bookshelf, this is an important space saving-tip to adopt.

This will help you store items in a flat position while freeing up more space. Also, you can avoid trying to fill up the awkward spaces left from storing furniture in their assembled form.

Dealing **with Pending Projects**

DIY projects are fun activities, but also time consuming. Due to the time you need to spend on a project, it is common for projects to extend over a few days, months, or years. These pending projects usually occupy space in your garage or shed. One of my friends has a two-car garage full of projects. Some are beautiful pieces of furniture, waiting to be refinished. Once, when we went shopping together, he wanted to buy a "cool" dresser he saw. Now, I knew there was one in his garage, waiting and lonely. We laughed as I said, "Now, how is your old dresser going to feel about this new, young model being brought home."

If you find old projects you started a few years back, now is the time to ask yourself a few questions.

- Will I ever continue this project?
- Will it remain unfinished forever?
- Is this something that I can realistically finish?
- Is this project taking up valuable space, and creating stress instead of joy?

When you give honest answers to these questions, then you can make the right decision – to discard or keep. If you don't have a timeframe during which you expect to complete the project, then it may remain unfinished.

Unstuff Your Attic/Loft

In comparison to your shed and garage, the items in your attic may often be unique. Often, we keep things stored in these areas that are considered important, or are seasonal - in other words, we bring out the holiday decorations just once a year, and in between we put them in the attic. Garages and other storage areas like this are often, also, places where we put things when we're moving to our new place – but, years later the boxes remain unopened.

In this section, I will introduce you to some of the things you may find in your attic, that may need to move out.

OLD PAPERWORK

These can be from your work, business, bills, or children's schoolwork. They include old letters, booklets, school reports, and more. Considering how difficult it is to handle paperwork just coming into the home, the challenge doubles when you have to go through old paperwork.

Another issue with storing paperwork in your attic is due to the dust and damp present in this room. Since paper won't survive under such conditions, you may lose the information on it. As we've mentioned, you might want to instead take photographs or scan the important information to keep it truly safe.

HAND-ME-DOWNS

The attic is the best place to store bags of hand-me-downs. These items quickly pile up in your home if people know you accept them. Although they're unwanted, they assume you need them in your home.

Unless they're actually useful to you, then you shouldn't be accepting hand-me-downs from anyone. You may be looking to get a toy or piece of clothing that will be useful to your child in a few years. This simple action is how you pile up clutter and create a mess in your attic.

You can also make an effort to donate these items to

charity if you're having difficulties getting people to stop sending these items.

PHOTOGRAPHS AND MEMORY Boxes

Everyone likes to look at old pictures now and then, but storing them in your attic isn't the best option. Similar to the case of paperwork, these can get damaged due to the conditions of this storage space.

Since photographs are often sentimental items, you must learn to discard them if you intend to free up space in your home. You can start by creating soft/electronic copies of these photographs to ease the process, as we've mentioned before.

You may decide to keep a few items in these memory boxes, but you must be thorough in your selection. You can put these items on display if you feel they are that precious. Other items in memory boxes should be discarded to create more room.

OLD ELECTRONICS and Appliances

We all enjoy a little bit of nostalgia. This is why we often hold on to our VHS machine or old cassette player. The problem is that you may never find any use for these gadgets in your home. DVDs, CDs, and online streaming make things a lot easier.

If you're piling up out of date electrical appliances in your attic, then you must take steps to discard them. You can find recycling centers to send these gadgets, or make extra cash by selling these items if they have any value.

The Takeaway

- Storage spaces in the home include your garage, loft/attic, and shed. Like every other space in the house, first, clear out these spaces when you decide to declutter.
- Look for duplicate items in storage spaces to discard and store like items such as tools together. Label boxes and containers in storage spaces to make things easier to find and create zones.
- Install shelves, hooks, racks, and clips for more storage and to maximize your space. Store sharp objects such as nails and screws in jars to prevent injuries.
- Dismantle furniture to make them easy to store and reduce the space they occupy.
- Discard the hand-me-downs and old paperwork in your attic; throw out old appliances.

9

MAINTAIN YOUR NEW GOOD HABITS

"Change might not be fast and it isn't always easy. But with time and effort, almost any habit can be reshaped."

— CHARLES DUHIGG

The decluttering process is one that doesn't end. You have to keep decluttering at regular intervals if you want to maintain a clutter-free home. Nonetheless, the habits you develop also have a role to play.

You must do your best to avoid going back to your old habits. So, what can you do to avoid your old habits?

Question Your Actions

The easiest way to go back to old habits is to fall for temptations. When you switch to the minimalist lifestyle, everything around you suddenly seems more appealing. The new store down the street, the beautiful watch you see on Amazon, and so on.

Marketers and advertisers will also seem like they're working extra hard. Well, they are if we're honest. These marketing and advertising companies invest large sums of money to get the right information on customer behavior.

They know how to stimulate you and influence your purchasing decision. That is how they sell their products. Since they're doing their job so well, then you must do yours. Your job is to decide if the product is useful to you or not.

You can do this by asking yourself these questions:

- Can you survive without the product?
- Does purchasing this product stray away from the minimalist path you have chosen?
- Will you experience any improvements in your life?
- Will purchasing the product have a noticeable impact on your finances?

These are some crucial questions you must ask yourself if you want to avoid falling for temptations. Answering these questions will help curb your impulse spending and help you maintain your stance on purchases.

Be Content

To ignore the temptations around you, learning to be content is vital. By being content, you can learn to silence the voices of marketers and advertisers desperate to get your money.

Knowing that you need to be content is the right step, but how can you achieve it? There are several ways to do this, and some may work for you, and some may not. You must discover what works for you. Here are some of the things you can do:

- Learn the act of gratitude
- Look inwards for the things about yourself that make you happy
- Identify little things that give you joy

Things you can be content about include your health, relationships, self-image, and so on.

Find Hobbies

Developing new hobbies, or engaging in previous hobbies is an excellent way to overcome your temptation and learn to be content. There are several hobbies you can try out.

The first is writing. Pick a book and pen, then start writing. Journaling is the most effective form of writing you can engage in at this point, and there are different types. Gratitude journaling stands out the most.

This is a form of journaling in which you write out

things you're grateful for. Through this process, you can improve your happiness. Writing by hand eliminates the need to type on your smartphone and is more fun than you think.

Reading is another hobby you can engage in. You can read newspapers, books, or magazines. The internet and platforms like Kindle offer a means to access books and read news online. Another great benefit of reading is the opportunity to develop your brain and exercise your mind.

Some newspapers or magazines provide brain games like 'sudoku' and crossword puzzles. Don't miss out on these opportunities for self-improvement.

If you have an interest in music, now is the time to show off your skills with an instrument. Rather than watching music videos, you can bring your family together and give them a performance. This will also help in improving your family bond.

For those that are still learning to play instruments, you can opt to go to a live concert. Seeing your favorite musician or band live has a lot more impact than watching them through your smartphone.

Another excellent option is to express yourself through painting. Nothing feels better than splashing a few colors to create a masterpiece. No smartphone app can give you the same feeling you get from using a canvas to help ease your anxieties and stress.

Go for a Feature Phone or Install Ad Blockers

Smartphones are the products of advancements in technology over the years. These advancements are some of the reasons why it is easy to fall for the temptation of advertisers.

One way you can curb this temptation is to go back in time. To do this, all you need to do is purchase a standard feature phone. These are the phones that have fewer features than the conventional smartphone.

You can also call these devices 'dumbphones.' Most of them have standard features like text messaging, making and receiving calls, and internet access.

These phones usually come with low storage capacity, lower processing capabilities and speed, and limitations in internet connectivity. They also lack the advanced multimedia capabilities present in smartphones.

Since these devices don't support most of the Android applications available, you can prevent yourself from opening any shopping app on your device. The internet connectivity on these devices is also less advanced so that you can avoid most of the ad pop-ups.

If you feel you still need a smartphone, then you can install ad blockers on the device. This will prevent you from viewing ads, but you have to put in extra effort to avoid going to sites like Amazon or eBay.

You could write a whole book on this topic – in fact, I have. So much of our world is numbingly distracting, and my book on digital minimalism might help you if you're struggling, like many of us, when it comes to our devices.

Avoid Things or People That Promote Spending

Some friends lead you on spending sprees. Avoid them at all costs. These individuals may ruin your life without them realizing it.

If you enjoy their company, then make sure you meet them in places like parks or restaurants where you're less likely to overspend.

If you have things that trigger your spending, then do your best to avoid them. These can be the sight of a shopping mall, the smell of freshly baked bread, and so on.

Plan Your Day

Planning your day involves following a schedule. When you keep to this schedule, you can increase your productivity while limiting your chances of slipping into old habits.

When planning your day, you must include essential activities you want to engage in. These activities are crucial in occupying the time you previously spent engaging in old habits.

There are lots of activities you can engage in, and regardless of the activity you select, it won't work unless you create the right environment.

To do this, be sure you're engaging in these activities without any distractions around you. If you want to stop using your phone before bed, then move it out of the bedroom and place a book on your bedside table. You're more likely to pick up the first thing you see in any situation.

Developing Healthy Social Network Habits

Depending on how you use social media, you can stray away from the minimalist lifestyle. This lifestyle promotes the idea of building relationships with those around you.

When social networks start doing more harm than good, then it's time to take action. Deleting your social media apps isn't always the best way to fix this problem. You can start by unfriending and unfollowing people on these platforms.

On social networks, you follow some users for the content they provide and not because you know them. These are the users you need to eliminate from your list. If you have a massive fear of missing out (FOMO), then you need to ask yourself a series of questions.

- How much information can you realistically go through every day without it interfering with your life?
- Is this information helpful or just for entertainment?

The idea of unfollowing and unfriending is to help you become more selective. Those you choose to follow should be those that have a direct, positive impact on your life.

You should also remember to unsubscribe from blogs and social platforms. All blogs offer an opt-in form to get users to sign-up. Once you complete this form, you give the blog permission to keep you up-to-date with their newsletters.

How many of these newsletters do you read? These newsletters often fill your inbox and pile up as unread emails. Start unsubscribing today. You can cut down your subscription numbers from 50 blogs to just five essential blogs.

When you go through the process of unfollowing, unfriending, and unsubscribing, you find out that you get to cut down your screen time effectively. Now, what can you do with the extra time you create?

One thing you must remember is that social networks are a way to replace real-life interactions. Therefore, you need to start hanging out with your friends more and inter-act, just like the old days.

When I say interact, I mean you should have a real discussion. A major problem you can observe when eating out is that a lot of people gather at a table and keep tapping on their smartphones. No one is taking the time to interact.

If you want to improve the quality of your relationships while reducing smartphone usage, get everyone to put their phones aside when you're hanging out. You can make things fun by setting a rule that the first person to pick up their phone has to settle the bill.

What Are You Really Buying?

This is a huge question you must answer if you want to maintain your new spending habits. For different individuals, buying goes beyond the exchange of money for goods. It can be a complex in their life.

This is common with compulsive buyers. Through their purchases, they can experience feelings of confidence, or think that they are gaining admiration from their peers. Sometimes a compulsive buyer is just using those purchases to get an adrenaline rush, sometimes known as "retail therapy."

If you feel a compulsion to buy anything you think you don't need, then you must use this opportunity to evaluate yourself.

- What is it you really want to gain from this purchase?
- Why are you falling for this temptation?
- Is there a void you're trying to fill?

Taking time to deal with the issues discussed in this chapter will help you overcome temptation in your daily life. These also improve your chances of maintaining a clutter-free life.

The Takeaway

- Developing new habits is crucial in maintaining a clutter-free life. Your new habits should address your spending habits.
- Questioning your actions can help in

protecting yourself from falling from temptations or traps to lure you to old habits.

- Learn to be content and find hobbies to distract you from old habits.
- Have a plan for each day, so there is no room for old habits to creep in.
- Develop healthy habits to address your social network usage.
- Learn about what you're buying. Is it the product, or a feeling?

AFTERWORD

Wow, you're here already? I am so glad you made it all the way. This is my greatest joy as a writer – thank you.

Throughout this book, I have extensively discussed the topic of decluttering. To achieve my goal of helping you deal with the clutter with your life, there were some essential concepts introduced. I know that some of this might be difficult, as decluttering our homes often means decluttering our hearts and minds. It's not as simple as it appears, and I make no judgment of you. We've all been there, and we're here to help each other.

Let's go back to the topic of "less is more." How can you apply this in your life? In what ways can you express the notion of minimalism in your everyday life, actions, words, emotions and in how you keep your home, car or office. These things sometimes seem unrelated, but really, they're not. Physical clutter is a symptom and one that requires deep work.

It's possible that you'll be able to quickly reorganize

your bedroom, bathroom or kitchen, for example. But, as we go through our lives, looking at what we hang on to and why can be a completely freeing activity. By letting go of things, and keeping life simple, we free up our lives, and we can move more fluidly through our world.

How will you continue on your new minimalist journey? You've taken the first steps. Which direction will it lead you? Will you choose minimalism in how you see your place in the world by exploring eco-minimalism? Will you move down the pathway of material minimalism? Technology? A combination of them all?

Unstuff Your Home is so much more than this book title. As you literally declutter, you may have difficulties, even with family members who may not be on board.

With the knowledge you have now, the next step is to continue on your minimalist journey. There are different types of minimalists, including essential minimalists, eco-minimalists, and so on. Have you decided on the kind of minimalist lifestyle you want to adopt?

On this journey, having people to support will be beneficial. The first place where you must start is in your home. Is your family on board with the idea of minimalism? Are your friends going to be supportive? Even though you might feel alone in this process, always remember that I'm here, as a friend, and as a support.

To remain by your side on this journey, I have several other books you might also find helpful. These books focus on how you live a simpler and more satisfying life. Some of these I've mentioned before. You might find any of them helpful. Titles include:

- Minimalist
- Declutter
- Minimalist Living
- Digital Minimalism

If you're taking your first steps to declutter, just by reading this book, you've already come a long way. I wish you the best on your journey of decluttering your life!

REFERENCES

Aitchison, S. (2017). 5 Reasons Why Less Is More. Retrieved 18 January 2020, from https://www.stevenaitchison.co.uk/5-reasons-less/

Armstrong, L. (2020). Dangers of Hoarding and Cleanup Procedures | RestorationMaster Finder. Retrieved 18 January 2020, from https://restorationmasterfinder.com/restoration/dangers-of-hoarding/

Avis-Riordan, K. (2018). Declutter: How to achieve a super-clean, organised & clutter-free bedroom. Retrieved 18 January 2020, from https://www.housebeautiful.com/uk/lifestyle/storage/a19562364/how-to-declutter-bedroom-storage-ideas/

Doland, E. (2010). Ask Unclutterer: Why do people struggle with clutter?. Retrieved 18 January 2020, from https://unclutterer.com/2010/09/17/ask-unclutterer-why-do-people-struggle-with-clutter/

Jay, F. (2011). Minimalism Around the World: Danshari. Retrieved 18 January 2020, from http://www.missminimalist.com/2011/08/minimalism-around-the-world-Danshari/

Oppong, T. (2018). Wabi-Sabi: The Japanese Philosophy For a Perfectly Imperfect Life. Retrieved 22 January 2020, from https://medium.com/personal-growth/Wabi-Sabi-the-japanese-philosophy-for-a-perfectly-imperfect-life-11563e833dc0

Palmer, B. (2013). How to Let Go of Inheritance and Gift Clutter. Retrieved 22 January 2020, from https://www.huffpost.com/entry/how-to-let-go-of-inherita_b_2903888?guccounter=1&guce_referrer=aHR0cHM6Ly93d3cuZ29vZ2xlLmNvbS8&guce_referrer_sig=AQAAAMXcvzOnSBYT_7zdCrjEF2RBeiea343usv_HNjC0NG2zWg404JdJZdwTzm1lQhbrvm9paFSkzJLgIvD4Cl8SjLJ5paBSd9IIba97BZAKXSOYOCaETR2bHyw9IonOrkoNAzs5tutw_Xl_wZRokZkcEuzSxTdleRpViuj9nnPlpdKX

Sewell, B. (2017). 6 eye-opening reasons why we accumulate clutter (and how to finally let go). Retrieved 18 January 2020, from https://increasingselfworth.com/6-reasons-accumulate-clutter/

THE END...ALMOST

Thank you so much for taking the time to read my book. I hope you have enjoyed reading this book as much as I've enjoyed writing it.

If you've enjoyed this book, please take a moment and write a short review. Reviews are not easy to come by.

As an independent author with a tiny marketing budget, I rely on readers, like you, to leave a short review on Amazon.

Even if it's just a sentence or two!

So if you enjoyed the book, please...

Help me out by leaving a brief review on Amazon.

I am very appreciative for your review as it truly makes a difference.

Thank you from the bottom of my heart for purchasing this book and reading it to the end.

On a side note, I have several action guides planned for the coming year and I have a feeling that you are going to love them.

If you'd like to be notified when I release them, and take advantage of early discount pricing, join my mailing list. You will receive my top 7-Day Declutter Challenge checklist to clean your entire house, in only 7 days!

Download your Check List Here:
https://dl.bookfunnel.com/jbyr5w8qpf

You will also receive my best minimalism tips via my email newsletter. I will show you how to make the most of your time and design a truly rewarding lifestyle!

Minimalist: The Ultimate Guide to Organizing Your Home, Decluttering Your Mind, and Creating a Joyful Life

Would you like to wake up everyday in a cozy and beautiful home, surrounded ONLY by the objects that inspire you to live a meaningful life?

Would you like to live a simple life with absolutely NO clutter, stress, or anxiety?

Discover: The #1 secret to Significantly Improve Your Quality of Life

>> GET IT HERE:
http://www.amazon.com/dp/B07VJY39GZ

AUTHOR'S NOTE

Thank you so much for taking the time to read my book. I hope you have enjoyed reading this book as much as I've enjoyed writing it.

If you've enjoyed this book, please take a moment and write a short review. It will help me a lot and keep me going.

Thank you for supporting an individual author like me, this really means a lot!

Warm regards,

Lilly

ABOUT THE AUTHOR

Lilly Nolan is a Cleaning Coach and Minimalist who is on a mission to help people declutter their homes and ultimately simply their lives. Through strategic organization, she ensures a harmonious space is created that promotes joy instead of stress.

Before she discovered the art of minimalism, she was overwhelmed by the amount of housework she had to do. No matter how hard she tried, she felt like she was running behind. Thousands of minimalism articles and books later, she decided to put everything she learned into action and immediately felt an unshakable sense of freedom. Before she knew it, Lilly became a go-to tidying expert.